A NEW DAY

JON SECADA
A NEW DAY

A CELEBRA BOOK

Celebra
Published by the Penguin Group
Penguin Group (USA) LLC, 375 Hudson Street,
New York, New York 10014

USA | Canada | UK | Ireland | Australia | New Zealand | India | South Africa | China
penguin.com
A Penguin Random House Company

First published by Celebra,
a division of Penguin Group (USA) LLC

First Printing, October 2014

LIBRARY OF CONGRESS CATALOGING-IN-PUBLICATION DATA:

Secada, Jon.
A New day/Jon Secada.
p. cm.
ISBN 978-0-451-46936-6
1. Secada, Jon.   2. Singers—United States—Biography.   I. Title.
ML420.S443A3 2014
782.42164092—dc23   2014015321
[B]

Printed in the United States of America
1   3   5   7   9   10   8   6   4   2

Set in Palatino
Designed by Spring Hoteling

This book is dedicated to Jose and Victoria Secada.
I am the product of their spirits.

CONTENTS

Contents

Contents

A NEW DAY

INTRODUCTION

"Happiness is never complete or permanent. You can work with what you have deep down inside to make your problems as unimportant as you can, so you can move on. Just feel good about who you are spiritually."

My father first gave me that advice during a particularly turbulent time in my life. I had reached a high point in my career, winning my first Grammy Award, while my first marriage was going down in flames. I hardly knew who I was anymore. Yet my father insisted on reminding me to keep trying and moving forward, even knowing that there will always be times of doubt and uncertainty.

As Cuban refugees, my parents instilled this thinking from the beginning. We had started from nothing, just clinging to the fierce resolve that our lives could only get better. Surviving meant embracing change with unwavering confidence, constantly reinventing yourself, and having the resilience to pick yourself up and keep going when life took unexpected turns.

My story is anything but easy. It is crowded with obstacles, skids, dives, and failures as well as success. It is a story about taking the opportunities that come your way and making the most of them, even knowing that disappointment, failure, and tragedy are also a normal part of life. The lessons in this book are ones I learned from experiences that tore me apart, lifted me up, and brought me back to the start.

It is true that happiness is never guaranteed—you will always face challenges that test your will. Strength is in finding what you are made of through hardships and your own fears and vulnerabilities. Wisdom comes from growing from those adversities. And resilience is built each moment of every day by constantly having faith in a new day.

PART I

From Havana to Miami the Long Way Around

CHAPTER ONE
Face Your Bullies

My heart pounded and my mouth went dry as my footsteps echoed on the cobblestones of the narrow street threading through my neighborhood in Old Havana, Cuba. I was about to walk into a lion's den. My tormentors would be lying in wait for me the way they did every day after school, ready to pounce. They'd call me names, chase me around, and threaten to beat me up.

I was just eight years old, short and shy and chubby. More than anything, I wanted to run away and hide. That had always been my go-to survival tactic.

But now my father, newly out of prison, was forcing me to confront my enemies. "I'm not going to let you run away from this," he'd scolded as we left the apartment. "You're not going to be bullied. You're going to confront those kids, whatever happens. I am not going to let you live in fear."

Easy for him to say! My father, Jose Miguel Secada, was a charming street guy, a hardworking, handsome hustler, in the best sense of the word. He seemed to fear nothing.

Dad had only an eighth-grade education, but he was keen on envisioning opportunities and taking advantage of them. He had grown up in a big family in Santa Clara, a village in the middle of Cuba, and he was a wonderful singer, like everyone else in his musical family. One of his sisters, Moraima Secada, even became an extremely popular international entertainer. Known worldwide as "La Mora," she was a member of the first female orchestra of America Anacaona.

My father could have become a professional singer as well. He had the voice and charisma for it. Instead, his passion was entrepreneurship. He was especially proud of his own father, who owned a pastry business. My dad worked alongside his father and had named me Juan after his dad.

Then my grandfather died, the pastry business went down the drain, and my dad was forced to leave Santa Clara to find work. He came to Havana with his mother, who died in his arms overnight of a sudden illness, leaving my father an orphan in the city.

Dad eventually worked his way up to owning an oyster bar, a small stand on a street corner in Havana, and saw opportunities to expand it. However, he was frustrated by the restrictions that Fidel Castro began putting on independent businesses when he assumed power in 1959. Chafing at having his ambitions reined in, my father saw his dreams going up in smoke as he watched Castro's regime strip away opportunities for entrepreneurs in the name of Communism.

Eventually, my father decided to leave Cuba. He would emigrate, and when he was financially able to, he planned to send for my mother and me. But his attempted escape by fishing boat to pursue his dreams was aborted when the authorities caught him offshore.

Emigrating from Cuba without permission from the government was considered an illegal act at that time. Families who wanted to leave Cuba had to apply for papers, and even then the government expected the head of the family to "give back" to the Communist Party first. As a result, my father was imprisoned and then forced into a work camp until the paperwork was passed for us to leave the country. He was in jail practically from the time I was a toddler until I was seven years old, leaving my mother and me to fend for ourselves.

My mother, Victoria, had an outgoing, loving personality and was also strong-willed. Like my father, she had come to Havana from Oriente Province, at the easternmost tip of Cuba, to make a better life for herself. She was a beautiful woman, Afro-Spanish as a result of her Cuban grandmother falling in love with a barber in the Spanish armada. Her father was also a businessman, but he died early on in a swimming accident. After her mother died young of cancer, my mother lived with her grandmother until she was fifteen. At that point her grandmother died, too, and she, like my father, became an orphan forced to make her own way in the world.

And so my parents—both strong-willed, good-looking, fiercely independent orphans—met, fell in love, and had me. My father had another family—an ex-wife, and a son and a daughter in their early teens—but I was my mother's only child, and therefore her driving purpose in life was to make my life the best it could possibly be. Meanwhile, my father saw his job as providing for us, no matter what it took.

While we waited for approval to leave the country, we lived hand to mouth in a small apartment near Paseo del Prado, the shady mile-long promenade in downtown Havana that dates back to the eighteenth century. Because my father was imprisoned, he was virtually a stranger to me. But my mother and I spent a lot of time together. I rode my little bike in El Prado park or went to the movies. We also spent a lot of time along El Malecón, the esplanade built to protect Havana from the surf that became the poor person's paradise, a favorite place to promenade or fish. When he got out of prison, my father tried to teach me to swim there in some of the little pools created by the rocks, but no matter how many times he threw me in, I never did get the hang of floating. I'm still a terrible swimmer.

In other ways, too, I was an outcast, which was partly why the bullies tormented me. I went to school close to our apartment, and my mother tried to protect me as much as possible from any brainwashing by Communist government propaganda, which had infiltrated the schools. I was small for my age but overweight, reticent to speak up in class, and terrible at sports. Although some of our friends supported our desire to flee Cuba, neighborhood committees monitored families that didn't adhere to Communist beliefs and did all they could to make you feel fearful and alienated as a result of not falling in line with Castro's regime.

In class, for instance, my teacher called my mother aside one day and said, "Your son is the only one who isn't part of Los Pioneros," the youth group established by Castro. The teacher explained that this was making me stand out as different, making it more difficult for me to make friends.

"How about if I just put the Pioneros emblem and the scarf on him for the sake of appearances," she suggested, "so Juan doesn't stand out as much? Then, when the group is finished with activities, I'll take the scarf off him. Would that be all right with you?"

My mother was torn, but for my sake, she reluctantly agreed. However, while that may have smoothed things over for me a little in class, it didn't help me in the neighborhood. We lived in one of the nicer buildings in inner-city Havana, but it was a tough neighborhood anyway. Many of the older, bigger kids saw me as an outsider not only because I was a shy, pudgy mama's boy, but because my father had openly declared himself against the government. Ambition had no place in Castro's Cuba.

So now here I was, deliberately walking toward my enemies,

unable to bail and run because I was even more afraid of displeasing my father than I was of the bullies in the neighborhood. Dad walked with me up the street until we drew near where the bullies typically hung out. Then he disappeared, ducking into an alley.

"I'm going to be close enough to jump in," my father promised, "but you need to deal with this on your own."

Dad gave me a stick to hold as he left me there. A stick, and a script: when the kids confronted me and issued their usual threats, such as, "Where are you going? You can't pass us!" I was supposed to reply, "Well, yes I can, because I'm going to kick your ass."

I couldn't imagine doing this. I was a dreamer, not a fighter. But I steeled myself against the attack and kept putting one foot in front of the other for the sake of earning my father's respect.

Slowly I went around the next corner. Sure enough, there they were. The big kids headed straight for me, shouting, "Hey, you can't pass us!"

Amazingly, something came over me. It was as if my father had given me a sudden infusion of his courage. I went nuts, completely berserk, running at them with the stick in my hand and screaming in rage and fear. "Oh yes I can!" I shouted. "I've got something in my hand, and I'm going to use it to make sure you let me pass!"

I was shaking with fright, but of course that made me look even more insane. My tormentors backed off and they never bothered me again.

My father had saved some money before he went to prison, and shortly after that incident we were able to finally buy our paperwork and airfare out of Cuba. Only certain countries accepted Cuban refugees in the seventies. My father had his heart set on emigrating to the United States, but since you could emigrate here only if you had family members who would sponsor you, we went to Spain instead.

On the day we received our paperwork, we drove to pick my

dad up from the work camp as the neighborhood committee and government officials confiscated everything in our apartment. They even took our "food book," where my mother had painstakingly recorded every food item we bought because groceries were so tightly rationed in Cuba.

The first two times we drove to the airport with our luggage, we were turned away—the government seemed to enjoy playing tricks on emigrants like that—and were forced to spend the night with friends in Havana because the officials had already locked up our apartment and removed everything we owned. We were essentially homeless, desperate to leave but at the mercy of bureaucratic whims.

We were turned away from the airport those two times. When we were finally given the word that our plane would depart, we returned a third time and boarded the plane to Madrid.

I was sad and scared to be leaving the only world I'd ever known. But as my parents led me up the boarding ramp to the plane, I felt a tiny flutter of excitement, too. My mother and father must have been experiencing a huge emotional upheaval as they went through the terrible process of giving up everything they had in exchange for freedom, but they made a point of acting and talking normally with me, enveloping me in a family safety net as a way of protecting me from the enormity of their own turmoil. They acted so matter-of-fact and poised as we headed into the unknown that an observer who didn't understand what was going on might have thought we were just going on vacation.

I knew better, though. I quietly took my seat on the plane and pressed my face to the window, watching Cuba recede as we took off, knowing that a page had turned in the book of my life. I knew this was it, the end of my life on this island. We weren't ever coming back. This thought gave me a hollow feeling in the pit of my stomach, but I was old enough to understand that it was our only choice if we didn't want to live under Castro's rule.

By leaving Cuba, I had learned my first key lesson in life: face your bullies. Whether those bullies are kids or an entire government, the only right choice is to stand up and make it known that you are your own person, ready to face even the scariest, most uncertain future.

CHAPTER TWO
Lay Stepping-stones to Success

We were nomads without a home. I vividly remember sitting with my parents at the airport and waiting for someone to tell us what to do or where to go, feeling slightly sick with anxiety.

Of course, we were hardly alone in the Madrid airport. Between 1959 and 1993, about 1,200,000 Cubans left the island. My family fled the country in 1970 at the crest of this wave of emigration. So many Cubans were emigrating to Spain that it was like a cattle call, with herds of Cubans landing in Madrid. As soon as you arrived, your family was granted 5,000 pesetas by the Spanish government to help you survive, but that was it. You were on your own.

Suddenly, someone out of the huge crowd at the airport recognized my father. This man had known my father in Cuba and was now living in Madrid.

"What are you doing here?" the man called when he spotted us milling around with everyone else.

"Well, we are here because we're here," my father said. "We left Cuba. But now we don't know what to do or where to go."

Our acquaintance gave us the address of a pension house and said, "Here, try this place. It's cheap enough that I think whatever money you have in your hand right now will cover your expenses while you get settled."

The pension house was in Old Madrid. My family could afford nothing better than a small, shabby single room. There was no bathroom to call our own, only a communal bathroom for the entire floor. Still, it rapidly became clear that living in Spain presented such luxuries, it was almost a born-again experience for all of us.

The freedom of having nobody telling us what to do, think, or eat, and the bounty of having so many different foods available, became immediately apparent on the cab ride from the airport. Peering through the taxi window, I saw fruit stands filled with oranges and bananas and lemons. There were even giant, brightly lit supermarkets! I felt thrillingly overwhelmed by the sight of so many choices.

As we arrived at the pension house and climbed out of the cab, I spotted a candy store. I had never before seen so much chocolate! I asked my father if we could have some, and we both ate so much chocolate that day that we were nauseated afterward.

It didn't take long for me to feel at home in our neighborhood. It reminded me in many ways of Havana, with its narrow cobblestone streets and ornate ironwork on the windows and balconies. Although I missed the pastel colors of Cuba and the tropical air, I was stunned by the grand proportions of the newer buildings in Madrid, and by the vibrant pace of life in such a prosperous city. There were tall buildings and fountains and people in bright clothes rushing about. There were even brand-new cars!

Despite this abundance, however, my parents were still immigrants with no connections, limited finances, and little education. They had to struggle to find work in Spain. My mother eventually found a few cleaning jobs. Each day after school, I would walk to wherever she was cleaning and wait for her to finish so we could return to our room together. My father couldn't find anything in Madrid. In desperation, he soon left Madrid for the Canary Islands to work in a resort as a cook—a skill he'd mastered in prison.

Thus began another period of painful separations for my family, as my father came and went from his job in the Canary Islands and my mother and I were left on our own in Madrid. Luckily, we were befriended by the wonderful family of *la portera*, the woman who managed the pension. Maria, her husband, Ramon, and the rest of their family and friends provided the comfort and warmth we needed to feel at home.

My parents fought for me to go to a private Catholic school, where I excelled and felt accepted. My mother and I also went to the central eating house set up for Cuban refugees by the Spanish government so that we wouldn't go hungry, and there we met other Cubans and rejoiced in the common accent and stories from home.

Because I was Afro-Cuban and darker-skinned than many people in Madrid, I was a fascinating creature to the Spanish kids, especially once they heard my Cuban accent. They wanted to know everything about Cuba, and I appreciated their friendly questions. I felt safe wandering around the new neighborhoods, like some sort of explorer discovering a grand, historic Europe.

I was not growing much taller or much thinner, though. I was still short and even fatter than before. I had always longed to be a baseball player, but since I didn't have the build or talent for sports, I began exploring my love of music. I had been surrounded by Afro-Cuban rhythms during my early childhood and must have naturally absorbed the musicality of my father's family. But since most of what you heard on Cuban radio stations was controlled by the government, the music I'd been exposed to so far had been limited in scope. In Spain, I began discovering pop music at a time when many male Spanish vocalists were arriving on the contemporary music scene.

This was the very beginning of my musical curiosity, as I listened to the radio and heard songs and voices that connected with my heart and spirit. In particular, I learned to love Nino Bravo, Raphael, and Camilo Sesto. Whenever I had the chance to be alone with the radio in my room, I'd close the door and sing along to pop music.

Nobody ever heard me sing, so no one had a clue that I was beginning my musical education—not even me.

After eighteen months in Spain, my father became frustrated by his inability to find enough work to make ends meet. We still hadn't met anyone who would sponsor our emigration to the United States, so he started methodically writing letters to the embassies of every country in the world that was accepting Cuban refugees.

We came close to going to Australia, where there was a government program that welcomed immigrants. That program included work placement, housing, and even education. A week before we were scheduled to leave, we received an unexpected response to one of my father's many letters: the president of Costa Rica had granted him a visa.

My father, who believed in his own abilities enough to demonstrate confidence no matter how great a risk he was taking, jumped at this new opportunity. "If I can establish residency in Costa Rica, I can claim you and you can join me," he told us enthusiastically.

So, once again, my mother and I were separated from my father. This transitional time was difficult, as my mother had to work extra jobs to support us. While we remained in Madrid for the next six months, my father traveled alone to Costa Rica and did what he did best: hustle. He found work as a cook in San José, and that job led him to meet another Cuban businessman who wanted to invest in a restaurant with him.

By the time we left Spain to join my father, I was ten years old. I was still introverted and shy, but I had made friends in Spain. I had been happy in Madrid and now felt the sharp pang of loss as we said good-bye to the city that had welcomed us. I knew we had to leave. At the same time, I wished with all my heart that my family had been able to make a go of things in Spain. I dreaded starting over. The only silver lining was that our family would be together again.

Soon after we joined my father in Costa Rica, our luck turned, thanks to Dad's hard work: he was ready to take one more leap of faith in his own abilities by breaking off from his partner, going to a bank, and asking for a business loan. He had spotted a little hole-in-the-wall restaurant on a cobblestone street in San Pedro, a neighborhood just outside San José and close to the University of Costa Rica. He and my mother could turn this modest space into a cafeteria. Finally, at long last, he could live his dream to become an independent businessman.

We all had to pitch in. I went to school in Costa Rica, of course, but every free hour was spent helping my parents at the restaurant, serving tables or working the cash register the minute my homework was finished. We worked long days. Then we'd all get up the next morning and work the same long hours again. I had no time for friends.

I am telling the truth when I say I didn't mind this one-dimensional life. Even then, at age eleven, I knew what a tremendous feat it was for my father to have opened this little restaurant. Plus, I had already absorbed the kind of work ethic from my parents that led me to share their drive to succeed. I was as proud and happy as they were when we were able to move from our tiny efficiency apartment adjoining the restaurant to a small house down the block. I felt like I'd helped make it happen.

My parents occasionally talked fondly of their Cuban childhoods and expressed a yearning for their villages or the people they had left behind, but they never expressed regrets about leaving the island. They were completely disconnected from what Cuba had become under Castro. For me, leaving the island had been like turning the page in a book, but for them it was closing the book entirely and putting it on a shelf. They were in exile and viewed that exile as permanent. They were fixed on looking forward and pursuing a better life.

The only exception to this was when my father received a letter informing him that Francisco, his son by a previous marriage who suffered from diabetes, had died suddenly due to surgical complications. I wish I'd had the opportunity to get to know Francisco, but I was too young to establish a connection with my half siblings before leaving Cuba. Francisco's death didn't hit me hard, but it was a devastating event for my father.

My half brother had been very supportive of what my father needed to do. Francisco had even written a letter to my father, saying, "I understand why you're doing this. You should follow whatever you have in your heart." Perhaps that made it even harder for my father to receive the letter about his son's death. It was the first time I ever saw Dad break down, and witnessing this made me realize again how much my parents had given up to leave Cuba and rebuild their lives—and mine.

Of course, working together from sunrise to sundown, plus living in close quarters after spending so much time apart, caused my parents to fight. They were both passionate people and had always argued, but now the fights were nearly constant and often reached a fever pitch. Their arguments were mostly about work or money, but sometimes they were sparked by my mother's jealousy over the attention my father paid to other women.

My parents had no choice but to fight in front of me. Our apartment was too small for them to have any privacy. I would retreat to a quiet corner and try to stay out of the way. The confrontations were loud and emotional, and occasionally my father would walk out.

But, no matter how heated the fight, he always came back, and the next morning we would open the cafeteria as usual and go back to work. Despite their differences, my parents did whatever it took to keep their business going, being very disciplined about working toward the common goal of achieving financial independence. I think all of us also recognized that we made up a tiny island, our little family of three. It was important to stick together.

Despite the fighting, there were certainly good things about being in Costa Rica. I liked school and I had started to make a few friends on the playground, even though there was no time to see them otherwise. Plus, the cafeteria was located near the University of Costa Rica in a neighborhood with lots of secondary schools. With so many teenagers coming and going, there was never a dull moment. Our modest little restaurant, where my father served Cuban-influenced cuisine as well as Costa Rican comfort food, enjoyed tremendous success. The place was always packed.

Because we were living and working near the university, my parents were also becoming increasingly attuned to the importance of education. We saw many students in our mini-restaurant and one of them, Manuel Costa, became a good friend. Manuel was a Cuban living in Miami who had come to Costa Rica to study dentistry. I was always a good student—I saw that as my responsibility to my family—and my parents now began talking with me about what I might be able to do as a professional with a university education. They even suggested that I might become a dentist like Manuel.

Despite our relative success in Costa Rica, my parents continued to view the United States as our ultimate destination.

America represented the holy grail of freedom, education, opportunity, and happiness. I knew it would only be a matter of time before they managed to set foot on American soil.

When I think about the sheer courage it must have taken my parents to pull off such a plan to leave Cuba and make it first to Spain, then to Costa Rica, where they struggled to save enough money to move to the United States, I am stunned by their willpower and determination. My father, especially, showed me how you can envision a future for yourself, then lay down the stepping-stones and use them to make leaps of faith to success, turning your dream into your destiny.

CHAPTER THREE
Seize Every Opportunity

After eighteen months in Costa Rica, my father sold his cafeteria. This gave us the financial freedom to buy tickets to the United States. Once again, I would have to start over in a new school filled with strangers, and this time I wouldn't speak their language.

In the early seventies, Cuban refugees who landed on U.S. soil could ask for political asylum even if they had already become residents of another country. We still had our Cuban passports, so we traveled as tourists. This wasn't an experiment, trial, or a vacation, however. Once again, my father had visualized our future and, with great confidence and determination, had worked hard to turn that vision into a reality. We sold almost everything we owned, packed up our few remaining belongings, and left Costa Rica knowing we were headed to our final destination.

By now my parents had made friends with other Cubans in both Spain and Costa Rica. Most of those immigrants, too, had settled on the United States as their ultimate dream destination.

Now we followed them to Miami and found an efficiency apartment in Hialeah, Florida, just one room attached to the back of a small house owned by another Cuban family. We had traveled the long way around, but we had finally arrived in the country we would call home for the rest of our lives.

My parents had barely managed to complete grade school in Cuba and spoke no English. Fortunately, southern Florida was a mecca for Latino immigrants, so they could conduct all of their business and social dealings around South Florida with other Spanish-speaking people. Unlike most of the other Cubans we knew, however, we had no extended family in Florida. We were completely on our own. Despite the language barrier and the lack of connections, my parents miraculously both found work immediately: my mother in a clothing factory and my father in a restaurant.

They were away for long hours, and this left me to fend for myself. I too spoke zero English on the day we arrived. Combined with my innately shy nature, this made me feel anxious, deficient, and isolated. I knew my only chance of survival would be to learn English as quickly as possible.

At first my parents tried to enroll me in a private Catholic school, but it quickly became clear that we couldn't afford the tuition. After a couple of months, they put me in Palm Springs Elementary School, which had a bilingual education program. They dropped me off once at the school, signed the forms, and then that was it: I was expected to navigate my way to school alone every day. I was held back a year, a standard procedure for immigrant children who were non-English speakers, so I was in sixth grade despite being nearly thirteen years old.

Of course, I was still one of the shortest boys anyway, and I was still overweight. On top of my struggles with English and the culture shock, this meant I was even more reticent about making friends, especially since I didn't play sports. I had never felt more alone. In Spain I'd had friends, and in Costa Rica I'd had my parents and felt useful in the restaurant. In this new life, in this strange land, my parents were typically already off to work by the time I woke up and they didn't come home until after dark.

I essentially became a hermit during that first year of adjustment, drawing into myself and avoiding any interactions with kids my own age. Whether it was because of the language barrier or all of the moving we'd done, my instinct here was to avoid contact.

With nothing to do after school, all I did was watch TV and listen to music on the radio. In a way, this turned out to be a good thing. If I'd taken a different path—say, if I'd fallen in with the wrong set of friends, or if I'd been noticeable enough to be bullied—my life might have turned out very differently. Instead, I became addicted to television, and TV was my best English teacher. I didn't understand a word on the TV shows, but I watched them religiously when I got home from school. I became hooked in particular on soap operas like *The Guiding Light*, because the roles played by different characters—evil women and virtuous ones, villainous men and heroic ones—were all abundantly clear even if the language wasn't, so the story lines were easy to follow.

I was also really hooked on game shows like *Family Feud*, because often they would flash the words they were saying right on the screen. It didn't take me long to begin associating the words I heard with the printed letters I saw. *The Carol Burnett Show* was a huge part of my childhood, too, because I saw it as the complete entertainment package; looking back now, I realize that watching that show probably sparked my interest in being on Broadway later in my career.

The radio remained an essential part of my solitary life, just as it had been in Spain. I listened to my favorite radio stations whenever I wasn't watching TV, with no desire to listen to any music in Spanish. Instead, I found myself drawn to American pop songs and imitating the singers to help myself learn English faster. In the early seventies, I was listening to everything from Elton John to Stevie Wonder, from Marvin Gaye to Barry Manilow. I made sure to copy the words and phrasings exactly whenever I imitated my favorite entertainers, trying to eliminate any Latino accent from my English.

My first musical purchase was a set of records that included a specific Elton John song: "Someone Saved My Life Tonight." I listened to that song over and over again, along with Melissa Manchester's "Midnight Blue." Later, I would have the privilege of working with Melissa, and one of the first things I did was tell her how much that song meant to me as a child feeling lost in a big new country.

With no extended family, my parents and I had to entertain one another on holidays. We loved driving to northern Florida, to St. Augustine, which reminded us of Old Madrid, or to Daytona Beach, where we were thrilled to be able to roar up and down the white sandy beaches in our little Dodge Colt.

My parents still fought a lot, but I was used to that by now. In retrospect, I think they stayed together partly because they were afraid something would happen to me. Without the three of us together, they knew I would feel more lost than I already was in this vast new country. They were committed to keeping our family intact.

My father soon had the money to open a cafeteria of his own. There began another period of long work hours for all of us, as my mother and I worked alongside him to make it a success. We followed this pattern for many more years. Whenever Dad got tired of a particular business, he'd sell it and take a break, then open another shop somewhere else. His success in business, as modest as it was, filled him with an exuberant energy. He loved being his own boss and approached each new business venture with a sense of invincibility. His driving spirit to succeed never wavered.

One of the first things my parents did once they had enough

money was to buy their own burial plots. "We want to make sure you won't ever have to worry about our funerals," my father said. They also took out life insurance policies with me as the beneficiary. Even in death, they were determined to take care of me.

By that time, I was a freshman in high school. I had survived junior high and I'd learned enough English to help my parents translate bills and school papers or tricky customer orders at the restaurant, although my mother somehow managed to make herself understood with Anglo clients.

I did well in school, and that was their barometer for my success as a child and theirs as parents. Besides, they were too busy working all day so they could put food on the table to worry much about what was going on in my emotional life. By the time I was fifteen, my parents even found jobs on weekends that took them out of town. I was left at home alone to soak up American entertainment for hours on end.

None of us had any sense that I was honing my musical sensibility or talent. However, looking back on that time now, I can clearly see that my musical education was ongoing as I sang along with my favorite performers on the radio or shouted out answers to questions on game shows, marveling at the exciting world of Anglo entertainment.

Although I never sang a note in public during that time, those early years in Florida represented the real beginning of my life as a singer. Throughout my early childhood in Cuba, Spain, and Costa Rica, there was something inside me that knew I could sing, but I was too shy and introverted to share that knowledge with anyone. I just kept singing on my own, imitating every performer as accurately as possible until American pop music had become a calling for me.

At the end of junior high, I had become even more self-conscious about my looks. I still longed to play sports and hated being so short and pudgy. I continued to prefer my own company.

Then, almost overnight, everything changed. My mother caught on to the fact that I wasn't growing out of my insecurity, and she made me go on a diet. At the same time, I started a physical education class with a real hard-ass of a coach. I'll never forget that guy's demeanor because he was the first person to push me. I thought I hated him.

"Listen, Juan," this coach said in his no-nonsense way, "you've got to get into shape and start competing out there with the other kids."

Every time I had his PE class, there was no messing around. He was a true disciplinarian and we all dreaded his class and the torturous activities he dreamed up. "He's going to kick my ass and I don't want to deal with this," I'd mutter every time I had to show up to that class, because it was like some nightmare of an Army boot camp.

Before long, though, I realized that, as horrible and sweat-inducing as those physical education classes were, I was starting to enjoy the exercise. Between that and the new diet, the weight started coming off. At the same time, I suddenly experienced a huge growth spurt.

Now that I was starting to feel better physically and inhabit my body more comfortably, I longed more than ever to play a sport—especially baseball, since that was the most popular sport in Cuba besides track and field. But there was no way to do this. For one thing, by now I was too old: all of the high school boys who played on the baseball team had started at young ages and were already highly skilled players. For another, my parents couldn't possibly support my participation in any sport that required money for equipment or transportation to practices. They worked nearly every hour of the day and barely had time to eat and sleep. I was on my own.

Finally, though, I discovered an extracurricular activity near my house that I could get into and that my family could afford:

tae kwon do. As I began taking classes at a studio within walking distance to my house, I rapidly became engaged not only in the physical workout but in the mental discipline of martial arts. And the more I practiced, the more powerful I began to feel as I gained the skills and control to protect myself and defeat an opponent.

By sophomore year, I was no longer overweight or the shortest boy in my class. That physical transformation gave me the confidence to start revealing my true passion—and some of my personality—through music.

I couldn't contain my desire to sing anymore; it was almost as if the music was bubbling over inside of me. I had seen posters all over Hialeah High School advertising auditions for the next musical. But I told myself I wouldn't try for that. I would just sign up for chorus. Even though I had no experience singing onstage, I had spent so much time mimicking songs on the radio that I felt sure I could do that much. I literally had a pep talk with myself, coaxing my shy, loner self closer and closer to the door of the music room one afternoon by saying, "Let's see what somebody else thinks of my voice."

The high school music teacher was in her room with a few other students when I arrived. The teacher, Ms. Van Antwerp, was a kind, nurturing Midwestern woman. Well into her fifties, she was very petite with dark hair, a warm smile, and big glasses. She was extremely welcoming when I walked into her classroom—which was a good thing, since I was shaking with fear as I took a deep breath and crossed the threshold.

Somehow I managed to find the courage to speak as I stood in front of her. "I want to sing," I said. "I thought I could join the chorus."

Ms. Van Antwerp nodded as if this was the most natural thing in the world, having a student just show up and announce his desire to sing at the end of the year. "That's fine," she said. "But you'll need to try out. Why don't you sing something for me?"

"What, right now?" I asked.

"Sure," she said. "What do you like to sing?"

After a little discussion, we settled on a Johnny Mathis song, "Misty." Ms. Van Antwerp played a few chords on the piano. As I started to sing along, she turned her head to look at me in amazement and said, "Who are you? And where did you come from all of a sudden?"

"Should I keep going?" I asked.

"Absolutely!" We finished the song together, and that small knot of anxiety I'd had began to loosen as Ms. Van Antwerp smiled and said, "Wow, young man, you can really sing."

That was the moment I knew I had to find a way to make music part of my life.

Working with Ms. Van Antwerp gave me my first connection to a music educator. In fact, it was my first experience with a teacher in the arts who was so welcoming that I felt like I could take risks in front of her and stretch my abilities.

"Okay," she told me, "from this day forward, we're going to do some things to make your voice even better. I want you to be in the chorus and to try out for the ensembles and for some solos, too. Are you okay with that?"

Was I okay with that? I had to laugh at the question, because honestly it was like suddenly being able to breathe after being oxygen-deprived for years. Everything I'd been absorbing musically since I was a small child had snowballed to a point where it was impossible for me to contain it, and now I had a way to let it out.

I spent the rest of high school being involved with music and theater. In addition to signing up for chorus and ensembles, I auditioned for the next school musical, *The Stingiest Man in Town*, a spoof of Charles Dickens's *A Christmas Carol*, and landed the role of young Scrooge. I also sang in the school talent show. I'll never forget that particular moment because it was the first time I'd ever sung in front of an audience. I had chosen one of my favorite Barry Manilow songs, "Daybreak," a song I learned by listening to one of his records.

I was so scared as I stepped onstage during the talent show that I was literally quaking in my shoes. But, when I opened my mouth, a funny thing happened: as I sang, I got such an immediate sense of gratification that I gradually grew more self-assured as the song went on. Afterward, I received so many compliments that my confidence soared even higher. At last I started to make friends as I discovered I wasn't the only one who loved music.

Junior year, I auditioned for the musical *Godspell* and was chosen to play the role of Judas. I was a little bugged that the role of Jesus Christ went to my good friend Miguel Morejon, but as Judas, I opened the show and had some great moments onstage.

Of course, what I couldn't know then was that my friendship with Miguel would far surpass my disappointment in not landing the lead. Many years later, Miguel would become my main songwriting partner, helping me write my bestselling hit "Just Another Day" and many other songs.

Miguel was instrumental in my development as a musician even early on, introducing me to bands and music I might never have listened to on my own. In high school, he encouraged me to take piano lessons, and it was Miguel who led me to rock groups like Led Zeppelin and Queen, saying, "Okay, I know you've been listening to all these solo artists and that's great, but you need to branch out."

I loved everything Miguel played for me. I loved every high school musical, every talent show, and even every choral performance. I loved music! I had always been a sponge, absorbing different types of music any way I could. Now I was actively grasping opportunities to improve my musicality.

My father's motto was take one opportunity at a time and

make the most of it. I was finally beginning to see that I had inherited his conquer-the-world spirit and sense of invincibility. Now I was following his example, seizing every opportunity to make my voice heard, not knowing yet where the music would take me.

CHAPTER FOUR
Open Your Heart to Change

I was a late bloomer in life in everything from launching my career to falling in love. I can hold only myself responsible for my career, but my father played a big part in an event that caused me to be extra cautious around women.

After having been a loner in high school, it was wonderful to finally make some good friends through music and theater. Even though I was clearly happy and busy, my father was worried about the fact that I didn't have a girlfriend, and he decided to initiate me in the wonders of womanhood. Soon after I turned sixteen, he informed me that we were going on a trip to Costa Rica without my mother.

"I need you to come with me to help take care of some stuff there," he said, talking vaguely about seeing a few business associates and handling some residency papers.

I thought nothing of it as we headed off to Costa Rica for a long weekend. The night before we returned to Miami, I went out with some old friends to see a movie. When I returned to our hotel I found my father in the lobby, hanging out at the bar with a few people.

"Hey, it's late," I said. "We should probably go upstairs and get some sleep."

"No," he said, "I'm going to stay here for a while. You go on up to the room. I'll be up soon."

"Okay," I said, and went upstairs to watch TV and wait for him to join me.

Somebody knocked on the door a little while later. When I opened it, I saw my father standing there with a woman. Even at sixteen, I took one look at her and knew by her outfit and makeup that she was a hooker.

"Look, *hijo*," my father said with a grin, "I think you know what you need. Have fun!" Then he disappeared.

The woman came into the room. She was in her thirties and immediately started trying to make me feel as comfortable as she possibly could, talking to me softly in Spanish while acting amorous. She had obviously realized right away what was going on, but she was getting paid to do a job, so she tried to do it well.

"Come on," she suggested sweetly. "Let's take a shower together. Wouldn't that feel nice?"

I was terrified—I'd never even kissed a girl, much less seen a woman naked—but I tried to go along with the whole scary scenario to save this poor woman, and myself, any embarrassment.

Ultimately, though, it didn't matter how much I wanted things to go smoothly. When it came time to perform, I couldn't do it. We tried to be intimate in a lot of different ways, but the technical feat of losing my virginity eluded me. The woman finally left and I pulled the blankets up to my chin, chiding myself for not being able to go through with what should be such a natural act.

Yet, afterward, when my father asked how it was, I felt compelled to lie. As always, I didn't want to disappoint him. "Oh yeah, it was great!" I said, and thanked him.

The truth was that the ordeal of trying to make love to that woman wasn't just unsatisfactory for me. It was horrific. I hadn't been circumcised, and the act of intercourse wasn't just complicated and uncomfortable, but was really painful for me. I eventually did tell my father the truth, but only many months later, which led to my circumcision to alleviate the problem.

In the meantime, high school was physically passion-free. I kissed one girl after getting drunk at a chorus party, but that was a bad idea in every way. Not only was I completely drunk, but after I drove her home, I vomited all over the car. My father was upset that I'd thrown up in his car, but he was easily mollified when I said, "Dad, I'm sorry, but I almost made it with a girl!"

The only other girl I ever took on a date during high school was the one I invited to the senior prom. Even that wasn't my idea, but the result of a dare one day at school when a friend said, "Go ahead. If you ask that girl over there to the prom, I bet she'd say yes."

I laughed at first, because my friend was pointing to the mayor's daughter, Robin Bennett, a beautiful blonde with blue eyes who was one of the most popular girls in school. Why would the beautiful blond daughter of the mayor date an ordinary-looking, poor Afro-Cuban kid like me?

To my astonishment, though, when I asked her to the prom, Robin said yes! I still remember the pleasure of driving to her house to pick her up, and how nice her father, Dale Bennett, was to me. All he said was, "You kids have a good time. Just be safe!" We had fun, talking and dancing the night away, but that was it: the sum total of my love life before college.

My parents were happy that I was involved in after-school activities and readily attended my performances. However, they saw my interest in music as merely a hobby. "We're glad you're getting such good grades," they told me. "Eventually, you'll be able to become a doctor or a dentist!"

Seeing how hopeful they were about my pursuit of a professional career made me feel increasingly conflicted as high school
graduation loomed closer. These wonderful new experiences in
music had ignited my soul, yet I couldn't imagine how to turn my
love for music into any sort of steady career. Plus, I certainly
didn't want to disappoint my parents.

Even as a child, it was my nature to always be analytical, reflective, organized, and prepared. These traits led me to excel in
school and graduate among the top ten students in my senior
class. I respected educators and I knew what an education could
do for you as a professional. In essence, the only two things I
knew for sure were that I wanted to attend college (though I had
no idea how to pay for it) and I wanted a steady income.

Reaching those two particular goals together while keeping
music in my life seemed impossible. What could I do?

Eventually, because of my strong connection with my high
school music teacher, it finally dawned on me that I could follow
her example and pursue a teaching career in music. While teaching wouldn't command the same income I would earn as a doctor
or a dentist, education was a respectable, steady profession that
would satisfy my parents.

At that point, I made a leap of faith and decided to find a college where I could study for a degree in music education with the
ultimate goal of teaching music at a high school one day. It never
occurred to me that anyone—least of all me!—could actually
make a living as a performer; I was simply settling for the most
practical way to make a living doing something I loved.

My guidance counselor and teachers encouraged me to complete the application for the University of Miami, knowing it had
the top music school in the country. Luckily, the pieces fell into
place and I was accepted with a financial aid package that included scholarships and loans. Immediately after high school, I
started my freshman year there, still living at home with my

parents to save money, but excited to be pursuing a college de-gree. I had even convinced Miguel to join me at the university.

My parents, meanwhile, were still fighting, arguing at top volume some days. It was clear that my starting college had caused a shift in their relationship. I had less time to help them out in the cafeteria, and they didn't have me around as much to buffer their relationship. One day, there was a particularly divi-sive argument, causing my father to storm out of the house.

I had to go out somewhere that afternoon. When I returned, my father was sitting alone in the living room. "Come here, *mi hijo*," he said.

He sounded almost mournful. I approached him cautiously.

Immediately, Dad started apologizing. "I've let you down, al-lowing you to see these fights," he said. "I feel terrible that your mother and I have been arguing in front of you like this."

I could see how regretful he was. "Pipo, it's okay," I replied soothingly. I didn't know what else to say. What mattered to me was that my parents were still together. My childhood founda-tion was secure.

I didn't know it yet, but my father was on the brink of a trans-formation, just as I was.

My joy at being accepted into a college with such a top reputation in music education quickly dimmed when I dis-covered how unprepared I was, compared to the other music stu-dents. I had sung with our high school chorus and I'd even had leads in school musicals, but the high level of talent at the Univer-sity of Miami was astounding. Yes, I could sing, but I had a long way to go.

The sad truth was that my musical education had started late in life. My talented classmates played instruments or had taken voice lessons all their lives. I had good, raw musical instincts and a powerful desire to perform, but that was about it. I couldn't read music very well despite my piano lessons, and I certainly didn't know anything about music theory.

To be accepted into vocal ensembles at the University of Miami required auditioning for placement. I appeared for one audition after another, singing my heart out as I tried to join a college group, but I suffered a humiliating rejection every time because I lacked the proper training.

The whole ordeal was almost enough to make me quit. Instead, I remembered my father's perseverance, steeled myself, and persisted. I reminded myself that my goal in coming to the University of Miami was to become a better singer and an educator. I needed to do everything I could to reach that goal and become the best music teacher possible.

Finally, on the very last day of auditions, I seized the opportunity that changed my life—and found the next stepping-stone to my career.

This particular day, I had decided to stop by the practice room for the jazz vocal ensemble. The other auditions had all been for groups that sang classical music, but the jazz singers did some contemporary music. I was still addicted to pop music, so that appealed to me.

The teacher, Larry Lapin, was alone in his room when I showed up that afternoon. He was a tall man with a full head of black hair, glasses, and a beard. He gave me a welcoming look and said, "Hey, man, how are you doing? What's up?"

I shrugged, terrified. "Not much," I mumbled.

He was very cool and immediately tried to make me feel relaxed, while at the same time feeling me out to find out what I wanted. "So, what brought you here today?"

I swallowed hard and said, "I want to try out for jazz vocal ensemble." It was tough to get those words out, because even as I said this, I was feeling way out of my element. A small voice inside scolded, *What do you think you're doing, showing up in this guy's room unannounced like this? This is college, not high school!* I wanted to disappear through a hole in the floor.

But Larry—as I would soon come to know him—just kept his cool and continued trying to make me feel at home. He sensed my anxiety and immediately switched gears, asking me questions about myself. More importantly, he made me feel like he cared enough to really listen to the answers.

"Okay," he said. "I'm glad you stopped by. Tell me what school you come from and a little about your background."

Soon we were chatting about everything from Cuba and Costa Rica to what kinds of songs I listened to as I grew up. Then he said, still acting very casual, "So, do you know any boleros? They're part of your culture, right?"

"I know a few, yeah," I said.

"Okay, that's great," Larry said. "Any particular one you like to sing?"

I thought a minute, then answered, " *'Tu Me Acostumbraste.'* You know that one?"

"Yeah, sure I know that one," he said. "Want to sing it for me?"

"Yes." I straightened my shoulders and took a deep breath. "Thank you, sir. I'd appreciate that."

Then Larry went to the piano—he was a well-regarded jazz pianist as well as the head of jazz vocal studies at the university—and played a few chords. "How's that? Is that the right key for you?"

When I said yes, he started playing the piano and I began singing along, feeling more confident as Larry started nodding in a positive way and saying, "Pretty good. That's pretty good!" Afterward he asked what part I'd sung in high school.

"Baritone bass," I said, my heart thudding in my chest. At that point, I still didn't know whether he was going to take me on or not.

Larry smiled. "Great. Come to the jazz vocal group rehearsal the first week of school and we'll figure it out."

I left the room feeling like I was walking on air. It was wonderful to be accepted. And by a college professor and a professional jazz musician, yet!

In terms of my musicianship, the jazz ensemble turned out to be absolutely the most challenging thing I did that first year of college. I remember walking into the first day of rehearsal, taking the sheet music Larry handed to me, and thinking it might as well have been written in Chinese. I couldn't read the music.

The other singers in the jazz group had no such struggles. As we all initially looked through the music, I discovered that my classmates were terrific sight readers and could interpret the music as easily as most people read printed letters on a page. I tried hard to fit in and stay cool, but I was scared I'd fail and be kicked out of the ensemble. For a few minutes, I even considered quitting before that happened.

But my ambition—that conquer-the-world spirit I'd inherited from my parents—overcame my nerves. I vowed to do whatever it took to stay in that ensemble. I grabbed the sheet music and headed straight for the music room. There, I spent hours carefully picking out each note on the piano, singing along to make sure I understood the music thoroughly enough to be prepared for the next day's rehearsal.

My ability as a singer grew during the first two years of college, and Larry became my mentor. Although I had declared music education as my major and never imagined making a living as an entertainer, I knew my true passion was performing. I couldn't deny that any longer.

I was in the right place at the right time: the University of Miami initiated its jazz vocal major my sophomore year. Larry, who was spearheading the program's initiative, approached me to see if I'd consider switching majors. "You'd be a great candidate for it," he said.

This meant a lot coming from Larry, who was living my

dream as a working musician in Miami. He had performed with jazz greats like Gerry Mulligan, Bobby Shew, Johnny Smith, and Sarah Vaughan, as well as playing regularly in clubs. I often went to see him perform at the Miami Beach Doral Hotel. My admiration for him grew the longer I knew him. I wanted to do what he was doing.

At the same time, I was still cautious. I knew a musician's income could be unpredictable. Despite the fact that my parents had accepted how committed I was to music and had stopped talking about me becoming a doctor or dentist, I was still living with them and witnessing firsthand how hard they worked to stay financially afloat. We moved a lot, always staying in Hialeah while trying to upgrade to slightly better apartments. My parents would work for a while in a cafeteria or restaurant, then continue their pattern of taking a break from working or looking for some new, better opportunity, always trying to improve their lifestyle. I knew how hard it could be to make a living. Did I really want to risk being a musician?

Despite these fears and doubts, the answer was yes. I saw no other path I wanted to follow. By junior year, I'd switched my major to jazz vocal performance. That decision changed everything. I had learned that I didn't just want to teach: I wanted to deal with every aspect of music, from teaching to entertaining, from arranging to songwriting.

My enthusiasm led me to become involved in a variety of different college ensembles and in anything else having to do with my major as well. The last year of college, I was even dabbling with teaching opportunities through different high school programs and outreach programs at a local community college.

Because of my accelerated progress in music and our personal relationship, Larry invited me to continue at the University of Miami as a graduate student in jazz vocal performance, with tuition and a small salary as his graduate assistant in exchange for helping him with the ensembles. I was honored; I would be the first graduate from the program and Larry's first graduate assistant.

If I couldn't make a living as an entertainer, at least having a master's degree would allow me to teach at the university level, I reasoned. Besides, on a profound level I was still growing and learning as a musician and a performer. Even though I was aware that getting my master's degree was kind of a safety net, it was one I enjoyed.

I could easily envision a future where I did what Larry and my other university mentors did, having a respectable, steady day job, in other words, while expressing myself through performance and songwriting. I saw no problem with working all day and all night. After all, that's what my parents had done, and I had absorbed their work ethic. A career was all about taking risks and laying down the stepping-stones to success.

Things were coming together for me now—even my love life.

By senior year in college, my confidence as a performer was growing, yet somehow that confidence didn't translate into a belief that any woman could possibly be interested in me. Bottom line: I was still too shy to ask anyone out.

For the most part, I had put the incident with the hooker in Costa Rica behind me, trying to erase it from my mind entirely. I didn't want that painful experience to represent the sum total of what it meant to be sexually active. I didn't want to just feel physically close to a woman; I was yearning to be emotionally intimate as well.

After what happened in Costa Rica, I had immediately retreated into my protective shell, focusing on keeping my grades up and absorbing everything I could about music. I suppose this felt natural, too, because I grew up as a loner. I was accustomed to spending long hours by myself whenever I wasn't at school, escaping into music.

Then, my senior year in college, everything changed. It was like being hit by a bolt of lightning. Our jazz vocal ensemble was on a road trip to a festival in Mobile, Alabama, and on the bus ride there I somehow fell into conversation with a classmate I'd always thought of as completely out of my league. This woman—I'll call her Samantha—was gorgeous and had a figure like a Barbie doll. I was intensely attracted to her, not just physically but because she was a fine singer and we shared a common passion for music.

I can't really explain why I had the confidence to talk with Samantha on the bus, but we connected there and during the jazz festival. The real eureka moment came days after the trip, as we got to know each other better and slept together for the first time. I couldn't believe how wonderful it was to be sexually intimate with someone my own age, a woman I truly was attracted to on every level.

Within a week, my life had transformed completely. Instead of immersing myself solely in music as I had done before, I spent every spare minute with Samantha. While this may have detracted from my studies for a while, being with her gave me the confidence to stop being so stupidly shy in other situations as well.

From that point on, I became more outgoing and assertive in social situations. And because I was more extroverted all around, I started feeling the attention from other people—even other women—as they sensed that I'd become more approachable.

Falling in love for the first time and discovering physical passion fueled my musical sensibility. I had started to write my first songs around this time, and it's fascinating to look back now and see how my songwriting career paralleled my urgent desire to be loved by a woman.

Despite Spanish being my native language, my instinct was to write songs in English. I suppose that was a direct result of the "sponge" process I'd been experiencing, soaking up American pop culture through radio and television since my arrival in the United States.

The first song I ever wrote at the University of Miami was "Wishes," an emotional, jazzy tune that I composed toward the end of junior year. This song coincided with the time when I started feeling really ready to have a girlfriend, and the lyrics expressed that longing clearly: "If wishes could come true, I'd spend my life with you."

I wrote "Wishes" as a jazz tune in the way Stevie Wonder is jazzy. The melody of the chords in that song is a combination of rhythm and blues, jazz, and pop; I was trying to balance a commercial sound with cool chord progressions that added depth. Afterward, I stepped back to listen to the song objectively and thought, *Hey, that's not too bad.* I still feel proud when I look back on "Wishes"; recently I even produced a new jazz recording of it.

After writing "Wishes" at the university, I recorded a demo of it, using the campus facilities. The song got positive reviews from my friends, so I continued to write songs for the next couple of years. I had effectively opened Pandora's box. I had opened my heart to love and to songwriting. And, like my father, I had to follow my heart and soul.

CHAPTER FIVE
Keep Hustling

Even before earning my master's degree, I was becoming one of the "go-to" male vocalists in Miami. I cobbled together a livelihood by teaching voice lessons at Miami Dade College, doing session work as a backup singer, writing songs, performing in nightclubs, doing specialty projects for Latin television, and taking gigs at night. And of course, whatever time I had left, I would spend with Samantha. I was sometimes so tired that my students would have to knock on my office door to wake me because I'd be passed out on the floor, completely exhausted.

With all of these different responsibilities pulling at me, I wasn't able to put in the hours I used to with my parents at their cafeteria. In my father's opinion, I was probably spending too much time hanging out with Samantha.

One day, he just went off on me in the restaurant kitchen. "You're living here for free, and you're not pulling your weight!" he shouted.

In the past, I probably would have backed down. I never

wanted to disrespect my parents and I was always cautious when my father was angry. But this time, maybe because I was already so tired and irritable from lack of sleep, I got pissed off.

"What do you mean?" I yelled back. "I help you out every chance I get!"

The argument raged on, with my mother watching quietly from a corner of the kitchen. Finally I'd had enough. "Look, if you're going to give me this much crap, I'm out of here!" I said.

More than anything, my father was the sort of man who refused to back down when challenged. The minute I said those words, he shot back, "Oh, really? Then get the hell out of here! You want to leave? Then leave!"

"Fine!" I growled, and started for the door in a red fog.

At that point, my mother realized I wasn't bluffing and jumped out of her chair. She was across the kitchen in an instant and hanging on to my arm, pleading, "Oh my God, please, son, please don't do this!"

I continued making my way out of the restaurant with my mother clinging to me. "Let go, Mom!" I said, trying to brush her off.

"You can't let him leave," she said to my father, crying hard now. Then, to me, "Please, son, don't do this!"

To passersby, it must have looked like some kind of comic B movie scene, with this woman clinging to her son for dear life. But I was beyond caring. "I'm sorry, Mom, but I have to get out of here for a while," I said, and managed to free myself from her long enough to get into the car and drive away.

The cafeteria was attached to the building where we had our apartment, and I had to return the next day to pick up some things. When I came back, my father was there. He had let go of his anger enough to apologize to me. "For your mother's sake, you've got to stay," he said.

I had cooled down as well. I knew he was right; it would kill my mother if I left. I was her only child, and a son at that. She had always made taking care of me her top priority, and she might have come across to some as traditional, in that she had only a sixth-grade education and spent all of her working hours either helping my father at the restaurant, taking care of our house, or socializing with a few close friends, and she did very little on her own. Yet she was a highly intelligent woman with a lot of common sense, and she was every bit as strong-willed and opinionated as my father. Maybe more so.

This was especially true when she wanted me to see that I was making a mistake about my lifestyle choices, like now. She did not want me to move out and she would move heaven and earth to see that I continued to live at home.

She also wanted me to break things off with Samantha. I would have said at the time that perhaps she acted the way she did because she was protective of me as her only son, and too attached to let me go. However, later I would see her behave in the same way with other women I dated when she sensed that it was time for me to let go of whoever I was seeing and move on, because I was wasting everybody's time.

At any rate, with Samantha my mother let me know right away, in no uncertain terms, that this girl was not for me. The two of them couldn't communicate—Samantha spoke no Spanish, and my mother kept what little English she knew to herself around Samantha—but my mother had made up her mind. "She just doesn't suit you," she'd say. "Break up with her. You have nothing in common," and "What do you see in her, anyway?" etc.

When Samantha was around the house, my mother never said anything blatantly rude, but her entire demeanor—usually so warm and welcoming—altered completely. Through her body language and expression, she spoke volumes, and was as alienating and distant as possible. She knew how to put up a really strong wall when she wanted to, and I knew it was her way of saying, "This person isn't for you. I'll help you make up your mind, Jon, because I know what's best for you."

I never called my mother on her behavior, but I soon stopped bringing Samantha around to the house. Still, knowing my mother didn't approve of Samantha was tough for me, especially because I knew she was probably right. I'd already started to notice other girls. I just didn't know how to end things with Samantha, since I'd never had a girlfriend to break up with before, and there was a part of me that still felt lucky to be with someone.

Our relationship had reached a rocky point by my senior year of college, when I had an accident driving home from a party with Samantha. To be fair, I think someone slipped something into her drink, but even so it was a horrific scene. We started fighting about something and she completely freaked out in a way I'd never seen her do before.

She really started telling me off, and in the middle of the argument she took off her shoe and began whacking me over the head with it. I was bleeding, but couldn't really pull over because we were on a highway.

"Stop it!" I yelled. "Knock it off! You're going to make us crash!"

It was no use. I couldn't control her, and I ended up doing a wheelie in the middle of the highway. The car slid over to the side of the road, and a few minutes later a cop passing by stopped to see if anything was wrong.

When the cop saw that I was bleeding and that my girlfriend was completely out of her mind, he asked us to explain the situation.

"I'm freaking out!" Samantha screamed at him. "Test him for drinking!"

The officer made me step out of the car and take a sobriety test. Luckily, I wasn't drinking and driving; even in college I wasn't much for partying.

"Test him again!" Samantha yelled. "He was drinking!"

Fortune was on my side. The cop just shook his head. "You'd better take your girlfriend home," he told me.

Not long after graduating, Samantha and I realized we really had no future together. She resented the fact that I had no time for her because I was performing in clubs almost every night, teaching during the day, and doing any kind of session work I could to get experience and earn money. She was pursuing her musical career as well, and there was just no way we had enough hours to share a life together. Plus, I had created a lifestyle where I was meeting all kinds of women in the clubs.

Finally Samantha called me one day and said, "I've had it. I'm fed up with you cheating on me and never having any time to see me," she said.

I felt terrible after we hung up, guilty and sad that the beautiful bubble of our relationship had to burst. At the same time, I knew Samantha had done the right thing. Things hadn't been working between us for a long time, and we were moving in different directions.

Around this time, I started seriously writing songs and entered a songwriting contest, El Festival del Sol de Miami. What attracted me to this particular competition was that one of the top prizes was the opportunity to make a demo album: one of the financiers had agreed to give the winner a hundred hours of time in his beautiful recording studio downtown.

The contest was marketed as an international one. While about ninety-eight percent of the contest participants wrote and sang their songs in Spanish, true to my history, I wrote and sang my song, "Return," in English. To my astonishment, mine was the winning entry.

Unfortunately, because this was the mid-eighties in Miami, I didn't get the opportunity to collect my prize of studio time. Especially in the music and entertainment industry, alcohol and drug use were rampant. It wasn't unusual to see booze, cocaine, and other drugs being trotted out even during working sessions in the music studios.

I have always tried to monitor my drinking habits, largely because my father made it clear that, in his family, alcohol addiction had been a problem. His mother was a party animal and loved to drink. And my aunt, the singer Moraima Secada, died from complications associated with liver failure as a result of her heavy drinking.

Drugs didn't appeal to me either, despite the fact that drug use was taken for granted among those living a certain level of lifestyle in Miami. I was brought up seeing my parents work so hard for everything we had that my inclination was to always stay on the straight path of discipline and sacrifice.

Unlike a lot of my musician friends and colleagues, I never thought drugs would help me creatively or extend my social circle, so I was always on the periphery in situations where drugs were a focus. And if things looked like they were going too far, I walked away. But most people who'd succeeded in the entertainment business at that time felt otherwise, including the owner of that beautiful music studio. Before I could claim my recording hours, the owner was arrested for drug trafficking and had to shut his studio down.

This was a huge disappointment. I had worked long and hard on that song, and that kind of opportunity doesn't come around very often. Yet there was nothing I could do but walk away and hope something better would come along. The only positive spin I put on the event was that winning the contest was still an amazing way to add another credit to my résumé as a musician. It would, if nothing else, keep my name circulating among people in the industry. Most importantly, this was my first connection with Rudy Perez, one of the contest judges, with whom I would have a lifelong association.

As I was transforming myself into a working musician, my father was making his own transformation as well. It took place over the course of three months and surprised us all.

We had never been a churchgoing family. I had studied and practiced with a friend who was a Jehovah's Witness in high school, but when it came down to being baptized, I realized there were certain beliefs I couldn't maintain and so I didn't go through with it. My mother believed in God, but she had no connection with any church. Neither did my father; his view tended to be worldly rather than religious.

One day toward the end of my time in graduate school, however, Dad asked me to sit with him in the living room. "Son, I have something to tell you," he said. "A few nights ago, in the middle of the night, I had a very special vision. I had an apparition and I knew it was Christ. He took over my spirit then and there. Son, I am a born-again Christian."

I was nearly speechless. Finally, when I asked my father questions about his experience, he told me that a regular customer at the cafeteria had seen him lose his temper. That man had given him a Bible and insisted that he start reading it.

"We read passages together," my father told me, "little by little, over a period of a few months. That's what led Christ into my heart."

Dad had experienced hardship all his life, and his anger came from a dark place. He had often lost his temper in shouting matches with my mother. Now, as he told me about his born-again experience and I reflected on my past few visits, I realized that he did seem like a different man. There were no more sudden rages. He wasn't even snapping at my mother. Instead, he seemed pensive and calm.

My father was in his late fifties by then. From that point forward, I saw him praying with increasing frequency and fervor. It was odd at first to see him go into such deep prayer. He occasionally even spoke in tongues. Dad was wrapped up in becoming the best Christian he could be.

At first I wondered whether I was ready to handle being with a father who was so drastically different from the one I'd grown up with, one who now held a fundamentalist Christian point of view. Gradually, though, I got used to it, and he seemed to settle into his own faith. I also saw how much his new spiritual approach to life helped his marriage to my mother. Instead of fighting about everything, he treated her with respect and held his temper, and over time, his desire to advise me spiritually would become a powerful force in my life.

Every conversation from then on would begin the same way, with my father saying, "My son, how are you doing? What's going on? I'm here to listen."

Remarkably, he did listen, too, with a new intensity, as I shared whatever was going on in my life. Afterward, Dad would say, "You must thank God and Jesus Christ for everything you have," and remind me that my problems were only as big as I made them. Then he'd offer me a few lines of scripture and pray for me. As always, my father was looking out for me, and knowing that made my struggles easier to handle.

I was fortunate that I was not only a bilingual singer, but that I was also in Miami, which had become a hub for major companies that were recognizing that their advertising campaigns needed to be in Spanish as well as in English. And because a lot of these multinational campaigns required unionized singers, my work with them was my introduction to receiving royalties for my work.

Musically, Miami was becoming a magnet for recording stars

of the highest level, especially those who recognized this city as the gateway to the Latin market. More and more artists were realizing that Miami was a happening place and a beautiful, vibrant, cosmopolitan city. New music studios were springing up like mushrooms, attracting not only musicians but top-quality producers and engineers.

One of the best-known pop groups to call Miami home was the Bee Gees. The British group had become international stars by the late 1960s, making their first appearance on *The Smothers Brothers Comedy Hour* in 1968 and writing hits like "How Deep Is Your Love," "Stayin' Alive," and "Night Fever" in the late 1970s. In 1983, the Bee Gees had recorded the songs for the film *Staying Alive*, starring John Travolta.

One member of the Bee Gees, vocalist and songwriter Barry Gibb, had also become a producer, using his Miami-based Middle Ear Studio to produce both his own recordings and songs for other artists. I was a big fan of his, so imagine my surprise and delight when the University of Miami got a call from a producer at Middle Ear Studio, asking if they had any vocalists who could translate English songs into Spanish, and I was the one recommended.

Barry Gibb had written a song that had already been translated into Spanish for one of his new solo albums; now he needed someone to help him sing it correctly. As I walked into Middle Ear Studio, I still couldn't believe that person was me! The first person who greeted me there was the great producer Joe Galdo, who would later end up working with Emilio Estefan as one of his initial producers for Gloria Estefan and the Miami Sound Machine. Then Barry Gibb walked into the room. I was only twenty-two years old at the time, and I really didn't know what to say or think about the whole scene, so I kept my mouth shut and let them do the talking at first. The reality was that I was scared to death.

Initially, Joe asked me to sing the song in Spanish while Barry listened, so that he could hear my accent and intonations on the song. As he watched me sing, I tried to focus on the music and my breathing to avoid being paralyzed by the fact that I was in the presence of a member of the Bee Gees, one of the biggest singing groups of all time.

Then it was Barry's turn to sing and I discovered the secret of his success: he was the consummate professional. As he sang, he kept asking my opinion.

"Am I pronouncing the words right?" Barry asked again and again. "I invited you here because I really need your help, as you can see!"

And whenever I corrected him, he'd do it over again. "How's that? Any better?" he'd ask. Actually, his Spanish was quite good, and with my coaching, his accent all but disappeared.

It was an amazing afternoon in every way. This was my very first contact with a major recording artist, and I was impressed by how warm and kind he was toward me, not only while we were working together but afterward as well.

At the end, as I was walking out, Barry turned to me and said, "Thanks, man. Hey, listen, any time you want to use my studio to make a demo or whatever, just call my manager, and if nobody else is using it, you can come here and record."

"Sure, okay," I said, nodding to be cordial and smiling at him, but all the while feeling sure that he was just being polite.

He must have known what I was thinking, because he stopped me and said, "No, listen, listen! I'm serious. Any time you want to, if the studio is available, come and do some demos if you can. You're welcome here. I really mean it."

I looked him in the eye then, startled and overwhelmed by his sincerity. "Thank you, Barry," I said.

I never did get a chance to use his studio, but that was a beautiful moment in my career. When I ran into Barry years later, I told him how much it had meant to me that he treated me with such respect and generosity, but he simply laughed and said, "I'm sorry, I don't even remember that day."

"I do," I said, "and I have to thank you. I came away from that day with a fond memory, knowing that someone of your stature could have his ego in the right place."

In many ways, Barry became one of my most important role models from that day on: a pop singer and songwriter who produced other artists and, no matter how successful he was, always treated other people graciously.

In the mid-eighties, Rudy Perez was known around Miami as a first-call singer who did a lot of session work and jingles. He was beginning to break through as a songwriter and artist. After getting to know me through the contest, Rudy would refer other people to me whenever he got really busy or, later, had work he couldn't do anymore as he moved on to bigger and better opportunities.

One day, Rudy called me to sing with Lissette Alvarez, a popular Cuban singer and Telemundo TV host married to Grammy Award winner Willy Chirino. Edito Martinez, Lissette's producer, wanted me to sing with her on a Spanish recording of the Bonnie Tyler song "Total Eclipse of the Heart."

I was actually really sick with a bad cold, but I jumped at the chance to work with Lissette. I did everything I could to heal my voice by the time the session rolled around. This would be my first opportunity to have my name as a singer appear on a record by a major recording artist, and I wasn't going to let it slip by.

International Sound Studio, where I'd be recording my vocals for Lissette, was located in North Miami Beach. (Later in my career, I actually ended up owning that studio for a while.) I arrived feeling simultaneously anxious and thrilled, knowing that how I performed on this one day could greatly impact my career.

This was a lot more important than just doing another jingle or bar gig.

Luckily, the session went really well. Lissette was wonderful to work with; since then, she has produced more than thirty albums, eight of which have gone gold. Whenever we've seen each other through the years, I always take time to tell her again how appreciative I was of that first big break she gave me.

As any working artist knows, the more people you work with, the more you meet. That's how careers are made. After recording with Lissette, I started to get even busier. When Rudy Perez moved on, I became the main male vocalist in town that Miami studios would call to do sessions like that. Besides working with recording artists, of course I was still doing jingles as well—songs in Spanish or English, advertising everything from pancakes to cruise ship lines. For some of these I had to sing the music by ear, for others I had to read music. Whatever I sang, I prided myself on my increasing flexibility and ability as an entertainer.

During this time, however, I also suffered a rejection that nearly broke my heart and made me question my abilities as a jazz vocalist. Just after finishing my master's degree in jazz vocal performance, I got a call to audition for Pat Metheny, a jazz musician and the leader of the iconic Pat Metheny Group. I had been a longtime admirer of Pat's because of the way his style incorporated contemporary and progressive jazz, jazz fusion, and Latin jazz.

Pat had also attended the University of Miami, so it was natural for his manager to call the University of Miami when they needed to replace Pedro Aznar. The university gave him my name, and when I got the call I was honored and nearly speechless with excitement. The opportunity to audition for this great international jazz artist—who would go on to win twenty Grammy Awards, along with countless other honors—represented everything I'd been working so hard to achieve. I saw this as the culmination of six years of study and, quite possibly, the launch of my career as a jazz vocalist.

Pat Metheny flew me from Miami to Boston, where his manager picked me up and drove me straight from the airport to the warehouse where they practiced. They had told me beforehand what to expect from the audition and what they wanted me to sing. In keeping with the habits I'd developed in college and graduate school, I had painstakingly transcribed the vocal parts to musical notation. I was determined to walk into that audition as prepared as I could possibly be.

Still, I was nervous. What if I blew this amazing opportunity?

Pat and the other four guys in his band did everything in their power to put me at ease when I arrived. Pat was totally sweet, a cool university cat with that famous dark mane of hair, a tall, lanky body, and a huge smile on his face. Pat's overall presence, then and today, was one of peace and tranquillity.

We did four songs, and everyone was complimentary about my audition. When we were finished, Pat said, "Man, you did a good job. You sounded really great. We'll be in touch."

I flew home, feeling relieved that the audition was over, but still uncertain about how I would measure up to other musicians who might be auditioning.

About a week later, Pat called me to say, "You had a good audition, bro', and I love your energy and your passion. Your intonation is like seventy percent there, but the thing is, I need it to be a hundred percent. Me and the guys, we love you so much, though, we want to fly you back to Boston again. That okay with you?"

We hung up, and I felt good that they wanted to hear me again, but frustrated thinking that musically I might not be up to par.

The second time I flew to Boston, I was less nervous. I performed as well, or maybe better, than I had the first time, but afterward Pat called to deliver the bad news. After thanking me for auditioning, he was kind enough to give me an excuse to explain why they weren't going to add me to his band, saying, "You're a great passionate singer, like I said before, but I've decided I want someone who can also play an instrument."

I was devastated. Deep inside, I knew what Pat was really saying: I wasn't proficient enough as a jazz vocalist to make the cut. That broke my heart. Everything I'd ever thought about myself—that I was the sort of trained singer who could one day make my living singing purely jazz—was forever changed from that moment on. Instead, I was going to have to become a more diversified vocalist and keep working on my musicianship.

Whether that was really true or not, it was my truth.

The thing I didn't realize at the time was that this rejection—like all rejections, really—would only serve to make me stronger if I put a positive spin on it. Somehow I managed to pull myself back together and do that. I reminded myself that I was doing what I had been put on earth to do: making music and helping out my parents financially, giving a little back to them after they'd given so much to me.

So I just kept stubbornly going forward, taking every job that came my way, whether that was singing jingles and doing session work as a background singer, performing in nightclubs, or teaching voice lessons. I also made a point of going to see live music any nights that I didn't have to work, because watching other entertainers was an education, too.

One of my favorite bands playing the clubs around Miami at that time was the Company, a Top 40 cover band. I was a big fan of theirs, not only because most of them were my colleagues from the University of Miami but also because I believed they were the best collective set of musicians playing in Miami, period.

One of the band members, Ed Calle, was a good friend of

mine. Around 1985, just as Ed was leaving the Company to do some touring, he talked the other band members into letting me try out with them, and it was a good fit. I couldn't believe my luck.

Joining this group led me to exercise my musicality in countless new ways. As one of the band's two singers, I was determined to perform at the same level as the other members. This band was so tight musically partly because everything they did was written down. They meticulously notated their songs, transcribing everything from drumbeats to chord changes and rhythm breaks, in a way no other band I knew of around town ever did.

The Company band members did this because they were all great musicians who were keen on making sure everything they did was musically visible on paper, to keep them on track and to allow them to replace somebody for a show if another musician bowed out. Because they were so exacting, everything the Company played sounded like it was ready to be recorded.

When I joined the group, I was so impressed by this practice that I started to do it, too. If I heard a song on the radio that either I or the band wanted to play, I'd write out parts for everyone in the band. The other singer in the band, Joy Francis, couldn't do the same, so I'd help her write out parts to her songs as well.

Singing and working with the Company was challenging, even difficult at first, but it captured everything I had studied and wanted to use in a working environment. I felt like I had truly found my place. I thought of myself as a team player, a musician like the other band members, even though my only instrument was my voice.

Now, when I think back to that first major rejection and the way I continued to hustle, I realize that it was the first time I'd had to seriously pick myself up, dust myself off, and keep going after my ego had taken a major beating. I credit my parents for giving me that ability to lift myself up after such a big disappointment. Despite the Cuban government trying to make them submit and then taking everything, despite the financial hardships and struggles they'd experienced in coming to this country, my parents had kept going.

"We're all only human," my father used to say. "We're all bound to suffer through periods of disappointment. But if a certain situation doesn't work out, you simply turn the page and move on."

That's what I did, and it had gotten me into the Company. I had achieved my goal of becoming a teacher and a working musician in Miami, making my voice heard.

PART II

A Working Musician in Miami

CHAPTER SIX
Believe in Yourself

Latin music was sizzling hot in the mid-eighties, and nowhere was it hotter than in Miami. The Latin explosion, and in particular the Latin music scene, meant that Miami was gaining an international reputation as a sexy, happening city and a serious center for the arts. José Feliciano and Julio Iglesias had shown that it was possible for Hispanic singers to cross over into the Anglo market. Feliciano and Santana, too, had been around for a while, but Julio started paving the way for Latin sound to infiltrate the pop market with his ballads and international appeal. He had a house in Miami, too, and South Beach was starting to take off as a desirable place to be.

But the two people who truly broke down barriers and set the stage for what the Latin music scene is today are Emilio and Gloria Estefan. A true visionary and the winner of nineteen Grammy Awards for producing, Emilio is considered the godfather of Latin music and responsible for shaping and developing the careers of some of the biggest and brightest stars, including that of his wife, Gloria, one of the bestselling artists of all time, and the most successful Latin crossover artist to date, winning seven Grammys. For them, it all started with the pop legend Miami Sound Machine.

Miami Sound Machine began as a local band with Emilio as its leader. The group started recording and releasing various albums on the Audiofon Records label and released their first Epic/Columbia album, *Eyes of Innocence*, in 1984.

What made Miami Sound Machine stand out was Emilio's relentless commitment to keep harnessing what the band represented in terms of the new worldwide interest in Latin sound. Eventually, that vision included putting Gloria in the spotlight as the band's lead singer, a position she truly deserved as one of the most talented, ambitious, and passionate singers around.

By the time I was performing with the Company in Miami, Gloria's star was definitely on the rise and shining bright. Her second English album, *Primitive Love*, had made her a true international recording artist, with three of the songs rocketing up the charts to become Top 10 hits on the *Billboard* Hot 100: "Bad Boy," "Conga," and "Words Get in the Way."

At that time, various neighborhoods around Miami offered opportunities to hear different sounds. You'd go to certain parts of town if you wanted to listen to Top 40 music, while other places offered salsa or jazz. The night Emilio came to see the Company, we were playing in a place called Raffles, a restaurant in what was then the Anglo section of North Miami Beach.

I didn't see Emilio walk into Raffles. He didn't make his presence noticeable; I think he wanted to make it appear as if he were casually dropping by. Still, word spread fast, and we were all excited to hear that Emilio—whose reputation as a musical entrepreneur was already on fire—had been in the club that night. The bomb dropped a few weeks later when Jorge Casas, the bass player, announced that Emilio wanted to hire every member of the Company except for me, Joy, and the drummer.

This was a cause for the band to celebrate. We had become good friends and I knew what this kind of lucky break could mean to their future careers. I joined in happily, despite my own inner panic about suddenly being left out in the cold. I understood that Emilio had come to the Company because he had specific chairs he wanted to fill for Miami Sound Machine: a bassist, a guitarist, a horn player, and so forth. He didn't need another backup singer, so he wasn't looking at me. I didn't have any hard feelings toward my friends, either. In their shoes, I would have done exactly the same thing.

Still, I couldn't help but wonder what I was supposed to do now. Singing with the Company had become my main gig, a mainstay of my income and a job I enjoyed. Jorge had told us what day would be their last, and that day wasn't too far away. If I wanted to keep doing these gigs, I'd have to hunt for musicians to fill the empty chairs in the Company.

What followed was a period of anxious scrambling, as the three of us remaining band members hired musicians to replace our departing friends. This was one of my early lessons in how the entertainment business works: just when you think you have things set up to your liking, somebody's going to pull the chair out from under you and you're going to fall to the floor. The only choice then is to give up or pick yourself up and find another chair.

After talking to my remaining bandmates, we all became the unofficial managers of the Company. Now it would be up to us to manage our bookings and income. I learned a great deal about the management process during this time, and realized how difficult it was.

Even while we were interviewing new band members and

getting the Company reassembled to our liking, I was still knocking on every door I could find on behalf of my solo career, hoping to land some kind of recording contract. I had finished a set of demos and wanted to shop them around.

In fact, they weren't really demos, but fully recorded, mixed, and mastered tracks that my parents had made great sacrifices to help me finance. By now, they had seen how completely invested I was in a career in music despite their worries about my financial stability.

When I thought the demos were as polished as I could make them on my own, I took them to what was then called CBS Records, the Latin division. This would later become Sony Music. There, I actually got one of the executives, a great guy named Angel Carrasco, interested in signing me. I felt like I was finally on the right path and on the brink of having my own recording contract, which was mostly Spanish tracks with a couple of English songs in the mix.

Even so, I didn't let up on myself. I continually asked the head of the department to give me more classes to teach, and I was performing every night. That driving schedule was nearly the end of me, too, as my exhaustion led me to the brink of death.

I was still making demo records during the day and performing as a background singer during session work, doing jingles, teaching, performing, and trying to keep the band together after the core of the Company left. This meant I was driving all over Florida day and night, as the gigs for the band were getting fewer and farther apart.

One night, I was driving back to Miami after a show in Homestead, a town about an hour from my parents' house. It was the middle of the night and pouring rain. At the time, I had a Mazda RX-7 and God must have been watching over me. The combination of speed on the highway and all that rain was nearly fatal: the car hydroplaned and I completely lost control.

The car did not just one but two 360-degree spins on the highway and slammed against the turnpike barrier. Luckily, nobody was hurt. A truck driver stopped to make sure I was all right, and then I slowly, slowly drove the rest of the way home.

That near-death collision made me realize how exhausted I was and how fractured my life had become, so when Emilio called shortly after that accident to talk with me about coming into the studio to do some work for him, I was more than ready to listen.

About six months had passed since Emilio had hired the other members of the Company; apparently, they had talked to him about me. They had told him about my technical skills and about my songwriting, too. He was now ready to think about expanding his production company and perhaps even taking on new talent to manage in addition to Gloria and Miami Sound Machine.

I had bumped into Gloria here and there around Miami, typically at some recording session or other, and we'd had a few casual conversations, but I'd never spoken to Emilio before this phone call.

"Hey, this is Emilio Estefan," he said. Then, without any preamble, he went on. "I think we can work together, Juan. How about if you come in and see me?"

I experienced a mix of emotions. I was beyond flattered that Emilio would call me—his reputation around Miami was growing by the day—but I had also arrived at a place in my career where I thought I was content. I saw myself as a working musician in the mode of the educators I respected so much at the University of Miami. I was doing exactly what I wanted to be doing.

I knew myself well enough to understand that, to work with anyone, I'd have to feel a certain synergistic chemistry. That person would have to share my vision of who I wanted to become as an artist.

The first person I called for advice after Emilio's call was

Jorge Casas. He was still working with Emilio and Miami Sound Machine since leaving the Company. He was also someone I really respected when it came to reading people in the business.

"So what do you think?" I asked Jorge after I told him about Emilio's invitation.

"Like anything else, it could be a good opportunity for you," Jorge acknowledged. Then he went on to say something my father might have told me: "Look, new opportunities are going to keep presenting themselves to you throughout your life, no matter what decision you make right now. Listen to what Emilio has to say, but take everything with a grain of salt and make up your own mind. Work with the opportunity you're presented only if it appeals to you. It's a very personal choice. Do your thing, keep realistic expectations, and take it slow."

That's still some of the best advice about the music business I've ever gotten.

At that time, Emilio's office was still in his mother's house in Miami. To be exact, it was a crowded space in her converted garage. The office walls were covered with posters and his brother, Jose Estefan, was Emilio's right-hand man at the time.

Emilio isn't a tall man, but he gives off waves of pure energy that's almost, but not quite, out of control. He's always had a full head of hair—it was dark then, but it's threaded with silver now—and he knows how to dress well. Emilio has always had a great sense of style, right down to his eyeglasses.

The entire meeting was a hurricane of information. Emilio laid out his vision for me, my career, and his studio in a single breath. That single breath lasted an hour. I was dealing with a musical impresario with the kind of blind-faith mentality and confidence to successfully sell anything he believed in. I had never met anyone like him.

That day, Emilio was selling his vision about his business

and my place in it. He showed me the tour bus for Miami Sound Machine, which was parked out on the street, and told me about the exciting tours and albums he was planning. He, Gloria, and the rest of Miami Sound Machine were combining pop sounds with Latin horns and percussion in a way that had mass appeal. Emilio was now at a point where he could afford to expand his pioneering production company, and he was getting phone calls from artists all over the world who wanted to work with him.

Emilio's intent was to sign new artists and to build up a company of songwriters and music producers. Members of the Company were his main producers. I would be the first new artist he would sign. Even more important to Emilio than signing me as an artist, however, was persuading me to join his production team. I had the depth of knowledge and training he wanted: songwriting skills, plus the kind of musicality that comes from being both a musician with an academic background and an entertainer on the circuit who had developed performing chops through practicing the craft by doing all of those jingles and nightclub gigs.

"Look at this tour bus," he said. "This could be the tour bus for you in the future! I think you're going to have a big career. You're going to be a great artist. But I think you should start as a songwriter. You can be a famous songwriter first, writing for emerging artists, and then you can have your career as an artist, and then a superstar, and have this tour bus. How does that sound to you?"

"That sounds pretty good," I said. In my usual way, I mostly listened, absorbing everything Emilio said and following Jorge's advice to pick through the avalanche of sound bites to see if there were opportunities here that made sense to me.

The thing that really got to me was Emilio's unwavering confidence. When Emilio believes in something—this is still true today—he believes in it so much that he will tell you everything right then and there about how he will bring his vision of the future into focus, laying it out from A to Z in a stream-of-conscious sort of unraveling that carries you along to that final destination.

Whether he was talking to the janitor, the president of Sony, or later, to my parents, Emilio always talked to people the same way, with charm and energy. He was so consistent in his enthusiasm that I knew he was spiritually connected to his ideas, even if those ideas sounded completely far-fetched to everyone else.

Throughout our conversation, Emilio did everything in his power to make me understand on a profound level exactly what he felt he could do for me. I absorbed it all with interest. Still, I was really torn. Gloria was also signed by the same label, CBS, that had recently expressed an interest in me as a singer. I had just finished my album for Angel and given it to him. I told Emilio this.

"Well, how deep are you into this deal?" he asked.

"I have a contract," I admitted. "And this record is coming out, I guess, or maybe they've already printed some copies."

At this point, I realized how powerful Emilio was, because he simply shrugged. "I think this particular record could harm you more than help you at this point in your career," he said, "especially since it's in Spanish. You need to get noticed first in the Anglo market with an album in English. Why don't I get you out of the deal? Let me talk to Angel for you."

That's when I knew that if I entered into a partnership with Emilio, it wouldn't be so much an agreement as a surrender. I would have to trust him to lead me if this partnership was going to work.

Signing with him would mean giving up my autonomy, but I knew that if anybody could sell what I did at that point as an entertainer and songwriter, it would be Emilio. I gave him permission to contact Angel, who very generously let me out of the deal with CBS, and I signed a management, publishing, and production agreement with Emilio. I still wasn't willing to give up any of my side jobs yet, but I knew I was in for an interesting ride.

That first meeting with Emilio will always stand out in my memory because I learned a valuable lesson: you have to believe in your own vision of the future, enough so that you can present yourself to people and sell them that vision. If you're going to risk everything for your dreams, the first person who has to believe in you is *you*.

CHAPTER SEVEN
Let Music Be Your First Language

Emilio rapidly began adding other musicians, writers, and producers as essential pieces of his production puzzle. I had been with him only a few months when he decided that his business was growing so fast he needed another space to house it.

Our new studio was in a former medical office building just four blocks from where my house is today. The day we moved into the building, there were only five or six of us; we walked in and immediately took over the little cubicles, setting up camp to work out song ideas. There was literally nothing else in the building.

Slowly, Emilio started constructing a premier production studio piece by piece. Watching how he grew his business, I appreciated what the production company represented and the collective creative talent of the people who were part of it.

My songwriting responsibilities started immediately. Emilio was acquiring projects from all over the world, and I now had the opportunity to team up with other writers to create songs for international artists. If I helped write something an artist liked, that song might be included in a particular project; if the project was then produced and became popular, I would earn royalties as a songwriter. If I received notice as a songwriter, I stood a better chance of making a name for myself as an entertainer.

That was a lot of "if's," of course. Those "if's" are exactly what make the music industry such a grueling, step-by-step undertaking: to be successful in music, you need enough creative passion and staying power to survive hour upon hour of relentless work to write, produce, and perform hit songs.

Emilio made it clear that he hadn't forgotten my desire to have a recording contract of my own. But he had his own ideas about how to go about making that happen. The first one startled me: he wanted to change my name.

One day Emilio called me into the office and explained that it would be better for me to start as an international English-language artist rather than as a Latin artist trying to cross into the Anglo market, as Gloria had done. "I think you should change your name from Juan to 'Jon' before we send out any of your demos," Emilio said.

I was taken aback at first, but after mulling this idea over for a few days, I started to come around. "Juan" was instantly recognizable as a Hispanic name, and the kind of music I was writing and wanted to sing was American pop music with infusions of rhythm and blues, and even funk.

I also trusted Emilio's sharp instincts when it came to creating an image. I'd seen how successful Gloria was. I had also seen how many changes she'd undergone stylistically to get to where she was at that point in her career. I always wrote songs in English, and if me having a less Hispanic name would help sell those songs and maybe even perform them onstage myself one day, then I was all for it.

Amazingly, my parents didn't seem to think that changing

my name was a big deal. They had become as invested in my career as I was, and they'd seen a lot of fellow immigrants change their names. From that moment on, my mother never called me anything but "Jon" and always corrected other people who made the mistake of saying "Juan."

On a day-to-day level, my writing skills were being put to the test. Typically, Emilio would come to us and say, "Okay, I have a big project here. We need songs for this artist. Anyone want to pitch something?"

These were assignment-driven projects. Emilio would explain what sort of songs the artist was looking for, then ask us to generate ideas. It wasn't long before I began to see a lot of development not only in my writing, but in the way I collaborated with others and began acting as my own salesperson.

Whether I'm writing songs for myself or for an assignment, it makes no difference: I've always been able to tap into a deep well within myself to access my emotions. The side effect of having had so much musical education was that I felt comfortable enough with my musicianship to try writing songs in different styles. I enjoyed the assignments Emilio gave me and saw them as a way to push myself creatively and professionally.

No matter what kind of artist I was writing for—or even when I wasn't writing for any project in particular—I made it a point to complete every song I did. I was determined to have actual demos of the songs I'd written on hand to play for Emilio whenever the timing was right. I was like some kind of superhero, walking around with this red case full of cassette tapes I'd made of my songs that I could pull out on the spot. Sometimes I even carried a cassette player.

Everyone wanted Emilio's attention; I carried the tapes so that I could take advantage of whatever few minutes of downtime we had around the studio. Whenever an opportunity arose,

I'd corner Emilio and say, "Hey, listen to what we did. Does this song work? No? Okay, how about this idea?"

I got used to pitching my stuff to Emilio with the same high level of energy he drew on to pitch to other people—especially executives at the big record companies. That was part of my growth process at his studio, and I'll be forever grateful to him for developing that hungry side of me.

Soon after I joined his studio, for instance, he handed me my first amazing opportunity. Emilio's production company had gotten a call from none other than an assistant to Don Johnson, the actor who played the lead in the popular *Miami Vice* television show from 1984 to 1990—yet another cultural icon that helped light up Miami on the world map. Don was recording an album, and his assistant was calling Emilio's studio to ask if they had someone who could help Don sing one of the songs in Spanish.

Jose Estefan negotiated the deal, then called me into the office and asked if I wanted to be the one to coach Don in Spanish. He named an hourly rate that astonished me, though it was probably only a hundred dollars an hour or something. When I agreed—in fact, I jumped at the chance—Jose said, "Okay, look, his assistant says they'll pick you up in a helicopter at a regional airport near your house. Just give me the address."

Soon I had the surreal experience of being carried away by helicopter to Star Island, off of Miami Beach. "Okay," I muttered under my breath as I grinned at the streets and houses growing smaller beneath me, "lifestyles of the rich and famous, here I come!"

Once we landed, I was escorted to Don Johnson's house—a glassy mansion, of course—where his assistant greeted me at the door. Then, all of a sudden, there was the man himself, coming forward to shake my hand and walk me into his studio. As we passed by the living room, I nearly passed out with excitement:

there was the actress Melanie Griffith, his wife at the time, who was no less beautiful or sexy in person than she was on-screen.

"Hey, Melanie, meet Jon," Don said casually. "He's going to help me with a song."

"Oh, that's great," she said, and paraded on by us.

Don was working on a duet with Yuri, the well-known Mexican singer. We went through the song for a while. When it was time for me to leave, he said he'd enjoyed the process so much, he'd like to work with me again. "Will you help me with my vocals for a few more sessions?"

"Of course, absolutely," I said.

Back home, I called the studio and said Don Johnson wanted to hire me. "No problem, man, that sounds great," Jose said. "Just keep track of your hours and I'll bill them when you're through."

I worked with Don in one of the studios in North Miami Beach over the course of the next week. Occasionally, I'd be hanging around the studio on my own because Don was filming and tied up on the set, but then he'd show up and work hard.

Once I'd finished the job, Jose Estefan sent Don the bill, which came to about $2,500 for my time. It wasn't a lot of money to Don Johnson, but it meant the world to me. We waited for payment, and waited some more. "Hey, have they sent the money?" I'd ask Jose every now and then, but the answer was always, "No, man, nothing yet."

Finally, Jose called Don's assistant, and then beckoned to me with a scowl. "I'm sorry, but besides the first few hours of that initial time in Don's studio, his management company and the record company don't want to pay the bill."

"What?" I couldn't believe this. "Come on. Are you serious?"

Jose was appalled, too. "I'm sorry, Jon, but they're being super unprofessional about this. We should let it go. Fuck him, man."

I knew it was likely that Don didn't even know I hadn't been paid, but I was still upset. How could he not know? I vowed that if I were ever in a position to tell him he owed me money, I would. I got that chance years later.

Meanwhile, I hung on to my freelancer's survival mentality. Despite the hours I was putting in at Emilio's studio, I continued working as a musician around Miami, teaching voice lessons, doing jingles and session work, and performing in nightclubs. Despite ostensibly being my manager now, Emilio never wanted any financial compensation for anything else I did for work; his interest in me was attached only to the songs I wrote.

I was content despite my hectic schedule and heavy workload. My ambitions had grown—I wanted better recording sessions, continued asking the head of the department at Miami Dade College for more hours, and I was invested in both songwriting and making demos—but I was managing my expectations, thanks to my university mentors. My professors had taught me to take a realistic view of the music business.

I constantly reminded myself that not everyone is supposed to enjoy a successful career in music. I might never be recognized as a singer or songwriter. I wasn't a rich man and I didn't think I ever would be. The important thing to me was that I was still following my dream, working as a musician and making enough money to pay the bills and help my parents. In my mind, I was a success.

I had been dating various women since leaving graduate school, and it was during this time that I met my first wife, Jo Pat Cafaro. We initially met at Miami Dade College, where most of my voice students were casual singers who signed up for private lessons. Jo was one of those; she started taking classes with me and eventually began frequenting Raffles, the club where I was playing with the new incarnation of the Company before Emilio called me to join his studio.

Jo Pat was a sweet woman, very approachable, extremely calm and easygoing. Looking back, I wonder if I liked her so much because, at least initially, we had a relationship that was steady and peaceful, unlike the turbulent marriage I'd seen my parents navigate. Plus, Jo Pat was beautiful: a dark-haired, voluptuous Italian American. We started dating and fell in love. Soon I was seeing her exclusively.

We seemed to have a lot in common. Jo Pat, like me, was very rooted in family values. She lived at home, just as I still did, and her family liked me as much as I liked them. I hadn't experienced such a close, trusting, emotional connection in quite the same way with anyone else in my life.

Something else that brought us together was Jo Pat's involvement in music. I was thankful that she appreciated music but wasn't as driven to become an entertainer as I was. She seemed content with her career as a beautician. At the same time, since Jo Pat's father and brother were both professional musicians, she understood my crazy hours. She trusted me enough to give me a lot of space. Even when I started working for Emilio and really going a mile a minute, I never felt any pressure from Jo Pat to make more time for her. And, when we were together, we enjoyed each other's company, going out to dinner or a movie, or to hear other musicians on my off nights.

So, when Jo Pat unexpectedly became pregnant after I'd been dating her for more than a year, I immediately asked her to marry me. I didn't give it a second thought. I just did it. I loved her, and I wanted to be the best possible father to any child I was responsible for bringing into the world.

Surprisingly, when I announced my decision to my parents, they were less than thrilled. They had met Jo Pat, of course, and liked her well enough—though the language barrier kept them from truly communicating, since they still hadn't mastered English—but they didn't understand my need to marry her immediately.

Part of that urgency was the result of circumstances. Not

only was Jo Pat pregnant, but my career had taken a drastic new turn: I was about to go on tour. And in Japan, yet!

One of the most interesting projects I'd been collaborating on through Emilio's studio was with Masayoshi Takanaka, a guitarist and international pop artist who was considered the "Carlos Santana of Japan." He was known for creating songs with a lot of unique rhythmic elements, and he'd chosen to work with Emilio in Miami because he wanted his next album to be infused with Latin sound.

Working with an artist of Takanaka's stature made me realize that Emilio's production company was gaining traction fast. I was pleased to be writing songs and doing some of the vocals for Takanaka, and even more honored to discover that he seemed to enjoy working with me as much as I relished working with him. He was an extremely easygoing, joyful musician, and I ended up becoming involved with every song on the new album he was producing for an offshoot of Sony Music.

When we'd finished the album, Takanaka returned to Japan. Within three months, however, he called Emilio to announce that he was planning to feature his Latin project on a Japanese tour and wanted me to accompany him and his band.

Emilio summoned me to his office after the call. "So, Jon, how would you feel about going to Japan?" he asked.

I was stunned. I had been on a college trip to Spain, but otherwise hadn't done much traveling since settling with my family in Miami. I'd certainly never toured as a musician. Going to Japan with Takanaka sounded about as exotic as touring the moon.

As if that weren't enough to make me feel anxiously thrilled by the prospect of working internationally, Emilio then dropped another small bomb at my feet: "The thing is, Jon, Takanaka wants to know if you could also play a little percussion. Naturally I said yes."

"Naturally," I echoed. I didn't freak out. Emilio knew that, like him, I would never say no to a good opportunity, even if it meant taking a risk and leaving my comfort zone—or maybe especially then.

"So you'll do it?" he asked. "You'll do percussion?"

"Sure," I said. "I'll figure it out when I get there."

The thing was, Jo Pat found out she was pregnant after I'd already agreed to leave on a three-month tour of Japan.

After I'd explained all of this to my parents, I said, "I really want to follow through with this. It's the right thing to do. I don't want my son or daughter to be born without us being a married couple and having that bond officially respected."

This, my parents could understand. They gave me their blessing, and Jo Pat and I excitedly made plans for an expeditious wedding. After we were married, Jo Pat would move into the loft apartment I had in my parents' house. It was all we could afford, and we agreed it was a good arrangement. Jo Pat would have people in the house to look after her if she needed it while I was gone.

A week or so before the wedding, I went with Jo Pat to one of her doctor's appointments. We were excited to have learned that she was having twins, and now that she was three months along, we were going to have our first ultrasound.

Jo Pat was in the middle of her exam when suddenly the technician said, "Oh, wow. Hmm."

Even though the technician immediately resumed her professional manner, saying, "Hang on just a second. I need a minute," as she left the room, Jo Pat and I both realized something was wrong. It was a scary few minutes as we waited for the doctor, holding hands and not quite looking at each other. My mouth was so dry I could barely swallow.

A few minutes later, the doctor came in and examined the sonogram. As I had feared, she shook her head and said, "I'm so sorry, but there isn't a heartbeat."

Jo Pat and I were both devastated. It was so surreal, excitedly planning to marry and become a family one minute, then knowing there was nothing to plan for the next. We went home and cried.

"Should we still get married?" Jo Pat asked me later that night. "You don't have to marry me now."

I squeezed her hand. "Of course I do. Let's do this. Let's get married. We'll have a happy day, and later on we'll have our family."

That, of course, was what I wanted most of all: a family. I longed to create a big, noisy family because I'd grown up in such a small one. I wanted that feeling of connection and warmth that you can only get in a family of your own.

It was a simple but beautiful ceremony. We held the wedding at a hall in Hallandale Beach, between Fort Lauderdale and Miami, with only our families and a few close friends present as we exchanged vows. I got married with no regrets.

The very next morning, I was on a plane to Japan.

It seemed like an endless flight to Tokyo from Miami. I traveled with another vocalist who had done the sessions in Emilio's studio with me; Takanaka had decided to hire us both.

Despite our jet lag and exhaustion, we went straight from the Tokyo airport to the studio where Takanaka's band was in the middle of a rehearsal. That's when I realized exactly what Emilio had gotten me into and started to panic. What followed was like one of those comedy skits where an actor is given a scene and a role to play, but has to improvise his action and lines. Imagine that the skit has something to do with pretending you're a surgeon in an operating room, or any other role requiring the authentic use of complicated tools, and you've got the general idea.

Everybody else was already in the room when I walked in and greeted the band. It was a beautiful rehearsal space with a full production setup. My percussion responsibilities—which I'd fantasized would involve playing a couple of bongo drums while I sang—in reality required a whole percussion rig: congas, bongos, timbales, cymbals, you name it. I even had my own technician. Takanaka was clearly expecting me to be what Emilio had promised: a percussionist as well as a singer. Yet I had never played percussion in my life!

Japan is where I learned that music truly is an international language. I didn't know how to communicate with most of the musicians except in sign language and a few words of English, but I managed to chat with the other band members for a bit while we prepared to rehearse. In the spirit of the gig I was being paid to do, I decided to just go with the flow. There was nothing else to do at that point.

"You happy with the percussion setup?" my assistant asked. "Anything else you need?"

"Yeah, yeah, I'm okay. I'm good to go," I told him.

We started rehearsing some of the songs. I knew what the real percussionist in Emilio's studio had done, so from a musical standpoint I understood the rhythms. Now I relied on my natural musicality and academic background to fake it, trying to hide the fact that I didn't have a clue what I was doing. I was like a karaoke singer in a bar mouthing the lyrics to a song.

Fortunately, I made it through. The Japanese culture is very respectful and welcoming overall, and Takanaka's band members were all friendly. Plus, the vocal things I was doing were so strong that whatever I was doing (or *not* doing) in the percussion department went unnoticed—or at least unremarked during that first nail-biting rehearsal! Only one band member spoke English, so most of us communicated through music instead of language, and the entire band was visibly excited to have me there, knowing I had cowritten the songs they'd been learning.

Maybe if I'd been a different kind of guy, the tour would have been a disaster. But making it clear that I wanted and needed the help of my fellow band members seemed to endear me to them, and they loved the music I'd written, saying, "Thank you for the songs, thank you, thank you" over and over. We also broke the ice by teaching one another swear words in Spanish and Japanese.

Once the band's drummer caught on and realized I wasn't a percussionist, he helped me out by showing me enough that I could at least get by. Everyone knew I was faking my way through it, yet on the basis of my personality and singing, they let it slide. I still don't know how I did it, to be honest. I was completely petrified. But I was determined to win these guys over and stay on the tour.

The band rehearsed less than a week and then got on the road, stopping in every corner of Japan over the next six weeks. Most of the audience members were in their thirties and forties, so there weren't any raging groupies or women throwing themselves at us. That was just as well. Being in front of an audience on tour was scary, especially given how self-conscious I was about my ability as a percussionist. This was also an eye-opening introduction to a different performance platform, one where I had to learn how to meld with musicians who were different from me in every way imaginable. I worked hard and prayed every day that I wouldn't screw things up.

Eventually I realized that, if I stuck to the drummer's script and copied what he'd shown me how to do, I'd be all right. To make up for my sketchy percussive abilities and lack of tour experience, I concentrated on my singing and decided to deliberately ramp up my performance personality. I had a few percussion solos, and whenever one came up, I'd imagine myself as an actor and give an exaggerated delivery, doing whatever the drummer had shown me, only bigger, maximizing my movements to great effect. The crowd loved it.

How you're perceived onstage is often a matter of how well

you entertain and connect with your audience, whether you're in a big theater or a small one. If you make a mistake onstage, I discovered, it's often much less noticeable if the audience is having a good time. It's almost always better to be too theatrical than not theatrical enough.

Being on that tour helped me break out of my shell even further. I learned what worked onstage and what didn't, instinctively assuming my performance personality whenever I took the microphone. I became a much more animated singer as well as a percussionist, and that enhanced everything I did.

I was also learning a lot about Japan and how to navigate my way through a foreign culture. I didn't know it yet, but those newly acquired navigation skills would prove to be invaluable to me later. We traveled by plane from city to city, and I loved the novelty of staying in the hotels.

It was an enlightening experience to view such amazing history, architecture, and natural beauty in Japan as well. I was especially moved by our stops in Hiroshima and Nagasaki, where for the first time I understood the horror of war from the Japanese perspective of citizens who were living in those cities when the bombs were dropped during World War II.

The other aspect of the tour I really enjoyed was the opportunity to experiment with different types of foods. After each gig, Takanaka would take the band out to dinner. I had never even seen some of the foods I ate on that trip! My favorite new discovery was shabu shabu, where you'd drop thin slices of steak and vegetables in broth right at the table and then eat it with your choice of different types of dipping sauces.

Because I'm of Afro-Cuban descent and certainly don't look Japanese, I got a lot of stares on that trip. I just smiled at everyone and enjoyed the attention. The language barrier was tougher; Japanese is a difficult language to pick up simply by traveling.

Still, we had our music, and the truly beautiful thing about music is that it speaks to everyone. A love of music is a powerful common denominator. Whenever the members of the band and I couldn't figure out how to communicate, we'd play a piece of music to get our meaning across. On that tour, I realized that music was my first language, and I could use it to connect with anyone.

CHAPTER EIGHT
Write Songs from Your Heart

After that first touring experience, I returned to Miami more determined than ever to make an album of my own and find more opportunities to perform. Before I left, I had given Emilio a set of five songs on a demo recording for him to pitch to record companies. I had cowritten the songs with the other guys in Emilio's studio and thought they showcased my various influences: rhythm and blues, Latin, jazz, and pop. I was excited to hear what a record executive would say about it and newly confident as a performer after my time in Japan.

Emilio took the demo to Sony Records because that was Gloria's label and he had developed good relationships with several Sony executives there. Meanwhile, I kept writing and working on different projects.

One day Emilio called me into his office. "I took it to the label and they didn't like it," he said bluntly.

My heart dropped as he explained that Sony was rejecting the label because the demo didn't have a unified personality. In other words, I was so diversified as an artist that it actually hurt me. I suppose the record executives couldn't figure out how to stamp me with a certain brand identity.

I was upset and disappointed, yes, but Emilio was furious. He couldn't believe that Sony didn't even want to sign a developmental deal with me, and he took the rejection personally. "Listen," he said, "in terms of your career as an artist, we can try this again with another company, or you can do a new set of demos and we'll try those somewhere else. But I'll also understand if you want your freedom. If you want to leave, I'll let you out of the contract."

My contract with Emilio was for five years, but it had been only three. I liked working with him and his team. Even if my solo career never panned out, I was writing songs and living my dream as a working musician. I had the flexibility to do session work, play gigs at night, and teach in addition to the hours I put in at Emilio's studio. I was hustling the way I'd always done and loving it.

"I want to stay," I told him. "Whether my career morphs into something else besides me being a producer or a writer or not, I'm totally fine doing what I'm doing."

That was probably the best decision I ever made in my life, because it led to working with Gloria on her next album—after the tragic accident that almost cost Gloria her life.

Jo Pat was still in school and working part-time. Unfortunately, the happier and the busier I was with my career, the harder things were for us at home. Somehow, whatever had led us to fall in love and get married now seemed to be evaporating as we tried to live together. We had never before spent so much time alone together, and it wasn't going well.

I blame myself for being too busy and distracted to really connect with Jo Pat and support her. I'd had the distraction of the tour to take my mind off the miscarriage, but my wife had been alone with her grief.

There was tension between us, but probably because I'd grown up watching my parents fight, I buried myself in work and avoided confrontations. I was burying the knowledge I carried deep inside, which was that I'd rushed into a marriage with someone I didn't really know as well as I thought I did.

It didn't help our relationship that we were living at my parents' house. Jo Pat had been living there while I was in Japan, of course, and as she and I started having problems, she and my parents began rubbing each other the wrong way. This was partly due to a lack of communication, but it was also my mother's way of beginning to wall herself off when she didn't like whatever woman was in my life. My mother always saw the writing on the wall about my relationships before I did.

I kept my head down and tried to survive my crazy work schedule and the tension between Jo Pat and me, putting one foot in front of the other to get through the days. Then, in March 1990, I got a call from Jose Estefan, Emilio's brother, that turned my world upside down. He was so upset that I could hardly make out the words. "Jon, there's been an accident," he said. "It looks like Gloria might be paralyzed."

I didn't know Gloria as well as I knew Emilio. She, Emilio, and I shared a common heritage and similar values, since we were all Cuban Americans who had immigrated to the United States with our hardworking families as children and we maintained our strong family ties. By the time I met them, the Estefans had had their first child, their son Nayib, and were somehow finding a way to balance their careers with a family life.

Gloria was busy touring to promote her *Primitive Love* album when I first joined the studio, so she was on the road a lot. When she did come into the studio to work on her own music, she was extremely focused and worked hard. As I got to know her better,

I ended up cowriting a couple of songs for her album *Cuts Both Ways*.

One of the things I admired most about Gloria was the fact that she always knew exactly what she was looking for in a song. Whenever we collaborated, she'd cut to the chase and give me her ideas, and I knew immediately whether she liked a song or not. She was never rude, only honest. In fact, although Gloria was an extremely warm, funny, personable woman outside the studio, whenever we were in the studio she dealt with the task at hand— whether that was songwriting or a vocal session—and she never brought anything personal into work, which raised the professional bar for the rest of us.

"Oh, show me something else," she'd say if she didn't like a particular melody or lyric. Or, "Maybe we can work on that some more."

Gloria was driven, intelligent, and never intimidating because she was such a warm person. Now, like everyone else who knew Emilio and Gloria, I was devastated by the news of her accident on every level—emotionally, personally, and professionally. A truck had run into Gloria's tour bus on an icy highway in the Poconos, and Gloria—along with Emilio, their son, and four other passengers—had been injured. Gloria had tucked her son into his bunk bed and was stretched out on the couch to watch a movie when the collision happened; she knew immediately that she'd broken her back in the accident because of the searing pain in her spine.

We were all thankful that nobody died in the crash, but worried sick about whether Gloria would even be able to walk again, never mind perform. The production company and studio froze overnight as everyone focused on Gloria's health. Some said it was a miracle that she got back on her feet as quickly as she did, but I think that was due to her determination to start her therapy and take it seriously.

Once a surgeon placed titanium rods in her injured vertebrae, with titanium rods, Gloria worked as hard at getting back on her feet as she did at everything else, putting music aside to devote the next months to regaining her strength and mobility. Her family, friends, and fans were with her every step of the way.

When Gloria returned to the studio, she was walking gently but with confidence. She went right to work. Emilio had already set up his production team to produce a comeback album to herald Gloria's return to music. I was excited by the concept and wanted to be part of it. I hoped to make an impression on Gloria with whatever songwriting ideas I put on the table.

It would be wrong to say I was writing songs specifically for Gloria, though. During the time I'd worked with Emilio, I had learned that it was best to write for the quality of the song, not for a specific singer. You can consider a particular performer's style when you're writing, but ultimately that doesn't matter. Songs are often produced and arranged in completely different ways for different performers. I'd learned that the most important thing was to always write the best song you can. The honesty of a good song will come through no matter who sings it.

Meanwhile, I was also careful to make myself as visible as possible while I was writing. Since I didn't know Gloria's schedule, I spent up to ten hours a day in the studio, making sure I'd be there even if Gloria poked her head in for an hour. And that's exactly what happened: Gloria became so accustomed to seeing me working in the studio that it seemed natural for us to collaborate on the new album. The writing came easily when I understood that she wanted to make an inspirational, almost gospel-like album with rhythm-and-blues melodies.

Gloria called her new album *Into the Light*. The name was meant to be a spiritual as well as a physical awakening, expressing how she was moving out of that dark time in her life. One of the songs that would become one of her biggest hits on that album,

"Coming Out of the Dark," came about as the result of Gloria, Emilio, and me working so seamlessly, so naturally, that it felt almost effortless. She'd come up with a melody fragment and I'd offer some lyrics, or I'd give her a melody and she'd write some lyrics for it. Within thirty minutes, the song was fully formed and written.

It's extremely satisfying as a songwriter to experience the kind of collaboration with another writer that feels like a cool, fluid process—a creative process that flows as if you and your writing partner are one person. It doesn't happen often. Gloria and Emilio recognized this as well, and we all understood that "Coming Out of the Dark" would be a powerful personal and spiritual anthem for her.

For me, creating that song made me feel as if I were in exactly the right place, doing exactly what I was born to do. That realization crystallized on an otherwise ordinary morning in 1991 as I drove my old Dodge Colt through downtown Miami on my way to Emilio's studio.

I had just stopped at a red light when "Coming Out of the Dark" started playing on my car radio. I was stunned both by the power of the song and by the fact that I'd written a song that was a pop hit being played on a radio station I listened to every day. Little did I know that this moment would mark only the beginning of my path as an international entertainer. "Coming Out of the Dark" proved to be not only a pivotal song for Gloria and Miami Sound Machine, rocketing to the top of the charts, but it blew the doors wide open for me as a solo artist. Today, even after twenty-five years in entertainment, hearing that song on the radio for the first time still represents one of the brightest highlights of my life, because that moment served as the first real proof that I might actually achieve my dream of becoming an American pop artist.

Even more significantly, in Gloria I had found one of the most important mentors of my life. She taught me the value of being in the right place at the right time, and the meaning of discipline and resilience, not only as an entertainer but as a human being. As Gloria made her way back to the stage after that devastating accident, she never lost sight of her passion for music, her love for her family, and her ability to balance her celebrity status with becoming the kind of warm, honest, giving person she wanted to be as a human being. I hoped to one day make her as proud of me as I was of her.

CHAPTER NINE
Learn from Your Mistakes

The minute *Into the Light* was released, the album started climbing the charts and Gloria began planning a tour. I had been overjoyed to hear "Coming out of the Dark" on the radio, and I was proud of the part I'd played in writing the songs on that album with her. I was equally thrilled when Gloria invited me to go on tour with her and provide background vocals with three other singers.

Looking back, I realize that Gloria probably invited me on the tour not only because I'd written many of the songs on the new album, but also because I was the only other artist, besides Gloria and Miami Sound Machine, whose career Emilio had decided to manage at that time.

For me, the invitation represented a fork in the road. All along, I had kept working as a musician while maintaining some career stability as an academic teaching voice lessons. Did I have the confidence to drop teaching and solely pursue a career in entertainment?

To complicate matters, a full-time, tenured teaching position had opened up at Miami Dade College, where I'd been giving voice lessons since my own university days. The department head said I was the front-runner for the job. At the same time, I was also offered a position at a small college in Illinois that was starting a jazz vocal studies program.

It was tempting to stay in academia. It represented a stable life-style, and I had always believed I would have a career in music education. However, when Gloria asked me to tour with her, I knew the only choice was to go. I could no longer deny my aspirations to be a performer. I turned down both academic positions, hoping to finally focus solely on my career as a songwriter and performer.

Gloria's new tour launched at the old Miami Arena. This was a big venue, seating around fifteen thousand people, but Gloria had no trouble selling out the seats since this was her hometown. I felt thrilled to be onstage with her, and with my old friends from the Company, too, who still served as the heart of Miami Sound Machine.

It was a blockbuster show. Miami Sound Machine had full rhythm and horn sections, and Gloria had added backup singers and dancers. We did four shows in the arena before hitting the international tour circuit, and I will always be so thankful and appreciative to Gloria for not only inviting me to tour with her as a backup singer, but for giving me what was perhaps the biggest lucky break of my career.

Gloria had several wardrobe changes during the show. As we rehearsed, she realized there was a moment when she didn't want to be onstage. During that moment, she said, "I want to feature you in a song, Jon."

My heart nearly stopped. I couldn't believe she'd want me to do a solo number. Not only that, but she wanted me to sing one of my own songs, "Always Something," a love song I'd cowritten while we were working on *Into the Light* that hadn't made it onto the album. I understood why. "Always Something" was about a conflicted relationship and how, as much as you try to work things out, you sometimes end up just going in circles.

Whenever I write songs, the emotions in them come from a real place. I had become a better lyricist as a result of writing so intensely for the past few months, raising the level of storytelling in my songs. "Always Something" reflects the downward spiral of my relationship with Jo Pat, which seemed to have sped up in proportion to the hours I'd spent writing music instead of working out whatever issues were threatening to shatter my marriage.

Jo Pat's needs and interests didn't fit into my ambitions, and so I continued to avoid her rather than face her disappointment in me. I knew my marriage was in trouble by the time Gloria asked me to go on tour. I think there was some small part of me that thought maybe getting some distance from the marriage might ease things between my wife and me. In any case, I chose to leave Jo Pat for an eighteen-month tour that would take me all over the world.

When it was time for me to take the spotlight onstage that first time, I was stunned and nervous, but excited. Gloria worked me into the show by first saying a few wonderful words about me to the audience, something like, "Listen, here's this Cubanito. I'm going to leave him with you for a few minutes because he's somebody I want you to hear. You're going to be hearing a lot from this guy someday. He's going to be a superstar."

Then she'd walk over to me and take my hand, leading me away from the other backup singers and onto center stage. There, I'd begin "Always Something" with this wildly acrobatic a cappella thing, starting with my chest voice and then going up to falsetto. It sounded really impressive when I peaked at my high notes. Finally the band would kick off on a high-energy rhythm-and-blues beat.

I moved all over the stage as I performed that one song, and people didn't just *like* it. They *loved* it, roaring and applauding when I finished! Eventually I even started getting reviews in the newspapers.

We went everywhere on that tour—the United States, Europe, Latin America—and no matter where we were, my performance elicited that same enthusiastic reaction from the crowd. I felt so blessed. Sharing the spotlight with Gloria was the culmination of years of hard work. She was one of the pioneers among Latin crossover artists, and I was getting to perform her magic onstage—and behind the scenes, too, joking around with the band. Gloria and I especially loved making up mock lyrics in Spanglish to our songs, something you can do only if you're a Cuban American raised in Miami. Because of our similar roots, our bond grew, and we were able to have fun and be ourselves together.

While all of that was wonderful, being on tour proved to be a bad recipe for my marriage. In Amsterdam, I met a woman after one of our shows with some of the other guys in the band. We were spending two weeks in Holland. This woman and I really hit it off, so I asked if she wanted to hang out with me, maybe show me some of the sights.

It was all innocent enough at first. She was from a city outside Amsterdam, and I told myself I just wanted to have fun with her. But this woman was so culturally and physically different from me that I developed a powerful crush on her. She had that kind of European flair in her mannerisms, and she was a tall, stunning blonde. My opposite in every way! We became friends quickly as we traveled around Holland together, and soon that friendship snowballed and she became more than that.

I felt nearly crippled by guilt the first time I slept with her. I had never done anything like this. What was wrong with me, that I thought it was okay to cheat on my wife? Was I becoming that lowest of the low, a musician who preyed on female groupies?

But it didn't feel like that, truthfully. I really liked this girl—I was a little in love with her—and I felt like I was having an adventurous awakening both emotionally and physically. This felt real. I invited the woman from Holland to meet me in other European cities.

Coming back to Miami for a rest during the tour brought the guilt crashing down on me again. Jo Pat had done nothing to deserve my infidelity. I felt terrible that I'd been unfaithful, and tried to make it up to her while I was home from the tour. I didn't tell her the truth—I'd always had an issue with confrontation, probably because I hated seeing my parents fight—so rather than admit that I'd been with another woman, I tried to make myself believe that I could work on the marriage and make things better.

No matter what I tried, though, I didn't feel any closer to Jo Pat. This was probably because I had deceived her and felt so bad about it. I knew our marriage was over, but I still didn't have the courage to admit it. I went back out on tour feeling even more estranged from my wife, and more affairs followed. While I was in Australia, I met another exciting woman, and she and I became intimate as well. I didn't recognize myself anymore. In despair, I thought back to all those times in Costa Rica when my mother had accused my father of playing around. Was I that same sort of man, who respected his wife so little that he couldn't stay away from other women? I was starting to feel worse and worse about myself—and yet I couldn't seem to stop my behavior.

Meanwhile, I was worried that not only Jo Pat but Gloria would find out about my infidelities. She and Emilio had come to my wedding and watched me exchange vows to love, honor, and cherish Jo Pat. I was compromising not only my own values, but Gloria's as well. Yet every time we flew back to Miami for a break between shows, I was so unhappy with my marriage that eventually I felt more comfortable being with other women than with my own wife.

Then the inevitable happened: Gloria caught me. We were traveling between Canada and the United States, and one of the women I'd hooked up with wanted to see me in Philadelphia. I made arrangements to meet her in the hotel, and when we got on the tour bus, we were all handed a rooming list for the hotel. I hadn't realized that everyone in Miami Sound Machine, including Gloria, would see that I was going to have a roommate in the hotel who wasn't my wife. I was mortified.

Gloria also spotted me hanging out with another woman by the pool in Venezuela. She gave me a little half smile but didn't say anything. It wasn't until the very end of the tour that she came down on me. Gloria had a tradition of having a big dinner with everyone and giving out silly awards after a tour was over. The certificate she handed to me in front of everyone read, "Most likely to be handed a paternity suit."

My stomach dropped and I couldn't meet her gaze, even though everyone around me was laughing. I'd never felt so embarrassed and awkward, having someone I respected and loved see the poor choices I was making—choices that could have terrible consequences.

That was my wake-up call. Soon after that, I confided in my father, who listened to what I had to say calmly, without judgment. "You have to find a spiritual place to work this out within yourself, and within the relationship you have at home, *mi hijo*," he said. "Obviously you can't keep living a double life. God and Christ will help you work things out with Jo Pat so you can move on."

I knew he was right. I also knew I should admit everything to Jo Pat. She probably had some idea of what had happened—she certainly knew I was doing everything in my power to put distance between us—but to Jo Pat's credit, she tried to be honest and face up to facts.

"Look, Jon," she asked me at one point, "do you feel like you need to see other women? I don't know what I'd do if you said yes, but I need you to tell me the truth."

I was a coward. Instead of leveling with Jo Pat, I followed my first instinct, which was to deny everything. "No, of course not," I said. I was prepared to live the lie a little longer to avoid hurting her, still hoping for some miracle to bring us together.

Given the success of my performance on the tour, Emilio had decided it was time for me to shine. He was ready to start pitching me to record companies. "If you're ever going to come up with another set of demos for me to show around to the record companies, Jon, this is the time to do it," he said.

Of course he was right. I needed to take advantage of this moment and seize my opportunity while the doors were open. But what was I going to do? I didn't have any new demos of my own, because I'd been busy working on Gloria's album and all of my other projects.

I knew I'd have to act fast if I wanted to step through those open doors. The first person I thought of was my good high school friend Miguel Morejon. We had lost touch with each other through the years, but recently a mutual friend had invited me to a party and Miguel was there.

Since dropping out of the University of Miami, Miguel had spent time doing production work focused mainly on dance music. He had gradually become disillusioned with the music industry, but we bonded that night and I asked if he'd be interested in working with Emilio. I recruited him for a couple of projects I'd been working on, just to help me do some arranging.

Now, before leaving for the European leg of Gloria's tour, I called Miguel and explained my dilemma. "I have to give the record companies something different than the demos I produced before," I said, "but I need to have my own musical identity."

Miguel promised to help me think through what that might be. I hung up feeling hopeful that we could form a songwriting partnership. Miguel knew me better than anyone, and he was one of the most talented writers I knew.

Ironically, even though I was worried about how I would get any writing done in Europe, it was during that part of the tour that I found exactly the inspiration I was looking for, as I experienced diverse cultures, met different people, and discovered new artists like Seal and George Michael. During a break in the tour, I returned to Miami and went to see Miguel.

"Listen, man," I said, "I really need your help. Remember what we talked about? I need to produce some demos and I have some ideas now for the kind of sound I'm looking for. I know we can do this. I just need you to help me put it together."

Miguel shook his head. "Look, I'm sorry, man, but I've decided I'm done making music," he said. "I'd love to do that with you, but I'm working in a flower shop now. I sold all of my equipment."

I was astounded. How could someone so talented give up something he loved just like that? Even if it wasn't for my own sake, I couldn't let Miguel drop out of the music scene.

"Come on," I argued. "This is our chance to do something together, something really important. Listen to this sound," I said, and played him Seal's newest album.

Even as I was doing it, I realized with a shock that I was pitching Miguel the way Emilio pitched everyone. I didn't care. It worked! I could see that Miguel was starting to feed off my energy. Encouraged, I kept at it.

"I know we can do this," I said, pressing hard. "I have a song I've written. I just need you to help me put it together."

Finally he grinned and nodded. "Okay. Let me see what I can do for you," he said.

When I came back from tour on my next break, I went to Miguel's apartment again. He had borrowed some basic equipment—a drum machine, a synthesizer, and a boom box—and he played me two pieces of music. We didn't use the first one, but the second sequence sounded terrific. That was the melody that would become my first hit song, "Just Another Day." This collaboration was just as seamless as the one I'd had with Gloria and Emilio while writing "Coming Out of the Dark": Miguel and I miraculously managed to write "Just Another Day" in half an hour.

Did we know we had a megahit on our hands? No way! But I could tell from Miguel's smile, and by the way he said, "Okay, that sounds pretty good," that this was a good, solid melody.

From there, Miguel and I continued writing together. We'd meet at his place and chat about our own lives first to get ideas for lyrics, using a notepad to jot down our thoughts as one idea sprang from another. For every song we wrote, we'd start by saying, "What's up? What's going on with your life?" Then we'd talk about our families, what we'd been doing lately, and about past and present relationships. Miguel would then play me a few tracks he'd been creating. After that we'd dig into writing lyrics as a result of our conversations.

Because Miguel and I were such close friends, it was easy for me to trust him and for us to reflect on life together. We shared our secrets and emotions not only through words but in melodies as well. Miguel was only the second person I trusted enough to confide in about my crumbling marriage.

Like my father, Miguel never judged me. He listened with compassion and understanding. He had met Jo Pat, of course, and at one point he shook his head and said, "You've got some serious decision making to do, Juan."

I knew that. More importantly, thanks to Miguel's friendship and his incredible songwriting talent, I was able to explore and express the seismic shifts in my life. All of my thoughts became lyric fragments and pieces of melody, rejecting not only my recent romantic entanglements and my failing marriage, but also relationships I'd left behind as far back as high school.

As a result, "Just Another Day" is evidence of where I was at that time in my life, a jambalaya of different yearning sentiments. The theme of the entire album that resulted was love, about the discovery of love and the disappointment love can bring us, about the poignant moments of couples together, about crushes and passions and future expectations. To this day, when my fans talk to me about that first CD, they connect with those songs because they hear the soul-searching infused into the words and music.

Meanwhile, writing those songs crystallized for me the fact that I was missing out on a deep emotional connection. "Angel," for instance, is the song I wrote for the woman in Amsterdam. From her, I took away a sense of having a tremendously positive personal adventure, one that needed to happen because of where I was in my life. I wrote "Mental Picture" for the woman I'd had an affair with while touring in Australia, trying to capture in music the exciting connection and romantic passion I'd felt during that experience.

As I wrote those songs, I understood even more that allowing myself to be unfaithful to my wife had been a mistake on a grand scale, morally and ethically. My usual method of coping was to shut down to avoid confrontation, and in doing so, I allowed the same emotional patterns that led to the end of my relationship with Samantha to destroy my marriage. Sometimes you learn more from your mistakes than you can learn any other way.

CHAPTER TEN
Happiness Is Never Permanent

Among the songs we wrote during that concentrated, emotionally exhilarating time for both of us, Miguel and I were most excited about one in particular, the one we saw as the title track on the album: "Just Another Day." However, Emilio wanted me to include at least three completed songs in my demo package. I worked with Miguel and two other writers, Tom McWilliams and Willy Perez-Feria, to finish the package in three months, patterning the production style of the other two songs after "Just Another Day" so the songs in the demo would all share the same musical flavor.

I put the demo together in a rush, in the middle of the touring process. Instead of calmly working through the final versions of the songs in the studio, I was forced by my time limitations to piece them together at my friend Freddy Pinero's house using an eight-track player in the living room of his apartment. Freddy is still holding on to those original tapes today. I knew that what the record company heard would be technically raw material, but

I hoped my performance on the demos would be enough to convince record executives that I had potential as a commercial artist.

Finally I handed the demo over to Emilio. He felt as enthusiastic about the package as I did and said he was certain he could sell it—and me—to a record company. Still, he went about things very cautiously. As always, the music business was like a chess game for Emilio, who always had strategies and backup moves. He knew when to be aggressive and when to be defensive.

At this point, he was on a mission to prove a point to the record executives who had turned me down at Sony Music. Gloria had signed with them, and Emilio's studio was involved in many different production projects with them; still, Sony had turned me down, and Emilio wanted to throw that rejection back in their faces. He took my demo package straight to another company while I was still on tour with Gloria, essentially thumbing his nose at Sony.

Emilio liked Nancy Brennan at EMI, so that was the person he chose to go to first. Nancy loved my demo and gave it to SBK Records, a new branch of EMI under CEO Charles Koppelman.

"We love it," they both said. "We'd like to meet Jon."

Emilio called me while I was still in Europe with Gloria. "We got a positive call, Jon," he announced. "I think we're moving in the right direction."

"Great," I said, stunned. "Really great."

At that point in my life, I had learned to take everything Emilio said with a grain of salt, so I tried to maintain an attitude of quiet confidence. We had been down this road before and made it to this point with Sony, and they'd turned us down. Emilio had been confident with that first set of demos, too, effectively saying, "We're going to get the biggest deal ever. Sony's going to love this project!"

When things didn't work out that way, Emilio pulled back a

little. I think he was trying to express confidence without getting me too pumped up; I was a very productive songwriter for him, so he was going to take care of me and proceed with a kind of protective caution. Still, I was thrilled even by the possibility that SBK might be interested in me. SBK had become the largest independent music publisher in the world, with Koppelman involved in the careers of entertainers as diverse as Michael Bolton, Robbie Robinson, Vanilla Ice, and Wilson Phillips.

I knew that SBK was getting serious about signing me when Nancy came to see me perform during one of Gloria's shows. Nancy and I felt a positive connection during the conversation afterward, which she ended by asking, "So, when can we have some more material?"

That was when I knew this was real. That was also when I started to get nervous. I didn't have any more material! I'd been too busy on tour to do much writing. Yet now SBK had fallen head over heels for my demo, and I had the green light to write more songs as Emilio started negotiating a deal with them on my behalf.

Emilio just shook his head at the Sony Music executives when they complained about him seeking out another label for me. "Sorry, but what could I do?" he told them. "Your Mr. So-and-so turned my guy down. We had to go someplace else."

The Sony executive who'd rejected me was eventually fired. Meanwhile, Emilio became a hero at his own studio: he had brought another major record label to his production company and was opening new doors for the artists who worked with him.

As thrilled as I was by the prospect of being signed by EMI, I was also immediately aware of the political nature of Emilio's risky move. At the end of the day, however, the most important thing to me was that somebody wanted not only the songs I'd written but me as a performer!

Everything—all of those "if's" in the music business—had suddenly fallen into place: I'd written a hit song with Gloria, she'd featured me as a solo singer, and I'd completed a demo that earned rave reviews from everyone who heard it. My shot at being a solo artist was definitely here, with all of the if's in my life finally spiraling in the right direction—some of them things I didn't even notice as they were happening. I couldn't afford to blow this opportunity.

The minute we had a positive reaction from the record company, the wheels started spinning faster. I was still on tour with Gloria, but I started to get little bits and pieces of information from SBK, like, "By the way, today so-and-so from the record company is going to come see you perform. He'll be talking to you about the other demos you need to complete when you're on your next break."

The first thing Emilio said after we heard the positive reaction by people at SBK was, "We've got to sign your friend Miguel right now, so he can help you finish this album."

Luckily, Miguel agreed to come on board officially. "Just Another Day" had whetted the appetites of the record executives, but we needed to complete this project if we wanted to sign a contract. Miguel went to town artistically. We already had something we liked musically, a blueprint of a song that people really enjoyed with "Just Another Day." Now he started coming up with different sequences as I finished out the tour.

We completed the next set of songs right in a row: "I'm Free," "Do You Believe in Us," "Angel," and "Do You Really Want Me." These were all songs that I cowrote strictly with Miguel, and they constituted the second wave of demos that the company heard. Miguel and I had a vision of what this record would represent thematically, and we stuck to it. The content of the lyrics had evolved and changed as we refined the music. Luckily, the people at SBK loved it.

I had one more hoop to jump through: Nancy's boss, Don Rubin, wanted to come see me perform and talk with me about this second set of demos. He flew from New York to England, and at that point, I allowed myself to relish the reality that SBK was serious about signing me and making my album a priority for the company.

The night Don Rubin flew to England to watch me perform, I was sick to my stomach with either intestinal flu or food poisoning. I had been extremely ill for the past twenty-four hours, and I was still so weak from vomiting that I thought I might pass out if I sang.

This is nuts, I thought, panicked. *This guy has traveled all this way to hear me sing, and my career is coming to fruition at just this moment. I can't be sick tonight!*

But I was. I was feeling about as bad as you can feel without dying, but I tried not to show it. I did everything possible to stay hydrated on the day of the concert in an effort to mitigate the effects of nonstop vomiting, but I still felt like crap—especially because now I was nervous besides being sick.

The other backup singers had noticed my predicament, and they all looked worried. I was being quiet, trying to conserve my energy. I knew they were freaking out about what might happen at that moment when Gloria would feature me, introducing me the way she always did by taking me by the hand during the medley of ballads she did in the middle of the show.

Just as Gloria grabbed my hand, I broke out in a cold sweat all over my body. *That's it*, I thought. *I'm going to have to just leave the stage or I'm going to pass out.*

I began to pray, communicating directly with any higher power that might be listening, saying, *Please, God, if you can just allow me the opportunity to make it through my solo, I would be so thankful.*

I was still sweating bullets. Just as the last ballad came to an end, though, I let out an enormous fart. I knew the other singers heard it, but they tried to act cool. For that moment, it was enough; passing gas relieved my intestines and I felt marginally better.

Gloria led me by the hand to center stage, as she did every single show, and I did my bit. I sounded good and survived the rest of the show even though I was still a little weak. I was even able to have my meeting with Emilio and Don Rubin, maintaining my professional persona by inwardly saying, "To heck with my stomach. I'll deal with it later!"

The meeting was full of positive energy. Don said, "Jon, man, I love all the songs you've done for us," and then he told me in detail what he connected to in each song.

This was the final test and I knew I'd passed it. From there, I continued the tour with Gloria and Miami Sound Machine, traveling through Southeast Asia and Latin America and everywhere in between. No matter where we went, someone from SBK would come hear me sing and introduce me to different affiliates of the company.

To this day, I'm glad Emilio was cautious in the way he presented me with news slowly, rather than pumping me up as he finalized the deal with SBK. "This is good," he might say, "but let's see what happens next."

"Really?" I'd say every time, always amazed that the good news kept coming. With him handling things in this quieter way, I was able to progressively take in the breaking developments between Emilio and the record company on my behalf.

In the fall of 1991, I officially signed the contract with SBK in my dressing room while I was finishing up the tour with Gloria. We were somewhere in the Philippines when Emilio came to me with the paperwork and said, "Look, it's ready to go. Here it is."

In many ways, it was the biggest moment of my career, a career that had already reached a level I'd never imagined achieving. But it was the most understated and surreal moment, too, because I was already touring and juggling songwriting with my travels.

After I'd finished writing my name, Emilio said, "Okay, that's it. We're signed."

This understatement belied Emilio's elation. Having me sign with SBK meant that his career was going forward fast. He had signed a Latino artist who came from nowhere to a big record label—a label that was going to market this artist to the mainstream Anglo market. Gloria had struggled to cross over to the Anglo market, and given those hardships, Emilio carried a chip on his shoulder. He knew how hard he'd had to fight to get to this point in his career. He was seeking recognition. When Emilio took me on board, Gloria was on the brink of being an international superstar, but he was still trying to prove himself. And now I was helping him do that.

Basically Emilio was saying to the music industry, "Look what I've done after all the crap you've given me about Gloria and Latin music all these years. When are you going to believe in the future of crossover music, and what I'm doing with this production company? I've brought you a talented artist who can sing in both languages. Now will you believe this is real and I know what I'm doing?"

For Emilio, this moment marked the beginning of a time when record companies would start recognizing the marketability of Latin artists and his production company would be the go-to place for breaking them out and developing their careers. He hoped these artists would knock down wall after wall in the music industry.

With me, once the deal was signed, Emilio was back to being his usual confidence-driven machine. He constantly laid out the plans as he envisioned them: "Okay, we're going to do this, and then this is going to happen, and I'm going to ask for this much money for your advance and we're going to get it, and I'm going to ask Charles Koppelman for a private plane from Miami to New York, and then a Concorde to go to France," et cetera.

For every decision there was to make, Emilio was ready to make it. He knew he had the upper hand because the company was into me. "You will always travel first class," he assured me.

Once we returned to Miami for good after Gloria's tour, Emilio had one more piece of advice for me as I was getting ready to embark on my own tour for "Just Another Day." Now that we had the contract, he said, "You're going to be taking pictures for a long time, Jon. For the rest of your career, God willing. I want you to consider fixing your teeth."

I trusted that Emilio had my best interests at heart, and it was true that my teeth were really crooked. So instead of taking offense, I decided to put blinders on and follow Emilio's advice and fix my teeth. I'd seen Gloria change her hair and clothing styles and figure. I had no problem fixing my teeth if this aesthetic improvement could help my image as a singer. I went out and got braces, and during the first set of photo sessions for that album, I just made sure to smile with my mouth closed to hide them.

I couldn't have been happier with my professional life, but my personal life was a different story. My marriage to Jo was all but finished, and I couldn't seem to put it back together.

By the time I signed the contract for "Just Another Day," my marriage was over. One night, I came home after a promotional show on a Miami radio station and found Jo Pat waiting for me. "Look," she said, "we have to sit down and talk."

"All right," I said, though I wanted to be anywhere but here at home with her. A knot of dread settled in my stomach as I followed her into the living room.

Once we were seated, Jo Pat shook her head at me, her dark eyes bright with tears. "I don't know why, but your feelings for me have changed, haven't they?" she asked.

"Yes," I admitted. "I still have feelings for you, but they're not strong enough to keep us together."

"Then I want out," she said. "I'm ready to make a move."

As sad as I felt at that moment, I also felt relieved that Jo Pat had the courage to say the words I'd failed to speak, but should have. "I'm sorry I've disappointed you," I said.

Jo Pat moved out immediately and started the paperwork. After we signed the divorce papers, I never saw her again.

Once again, my father was the one who helped me the most during this turmoil. "Look, Jon, God didn't put us on this earth to be miserable," he said. "Happiness is neither complete nor permanent. You experience it in bits and pieces. The rest of the time, you deal with your problems, whatever they may be, because your problems are only ever as big as you make them. You need to work to live and experience those happy moments as much as you can. Learn from this and move on."

His wise words were a gift to me at that time, and they still hold true today. I had made mistakes and they'd caught up with me. I could only hope that I could genuinely learn from those mistakes, manage my problems, and find a way to keep experiencing happiness. Meanwhile, my career had gone into high gear as I began promoting my first album.

CHAPTER ELEVEN
Be a Team Player

By the time the tour with Gloria was officially over, I'd chosen the final songs to complete my first album, *Jon Secada*, in 1992. I was extremely lucky to land Phil Ramone to produce "Just Another Day" as the first single, as well as "Angel." Clay Ostwald and Jorge Casas, two of my friends who'd produced a lot of Gloria's music, did the rest. We finished the album in four months.

I had a decent budget and was in an extremely fortunate position. SBK was making it clear that I was a priority artist and they were giving me a lot of attention and marketing dollars.

The fact that SBK was heavily invested in my career was hammered home by the president of the company, Charles Koppelman, when he invited me to New York to meet the team that would be producing and promoting my album. Emilio wanted me to walk into those meetings looking and feeling like a star, so he helped me buy an Armani suit and had it tailored to fit me perfectly. He chose a very businesslike pin-striped blue suit and a white shirt with a little pattern to give it some extra punch. I'd never worn anything that sharp.

I was glad to be wearing that suit when we arrived at the SBK offices on the Avenue of the Americas in New York City. My new look allowed me to stride into those meetings feeling like a Frank Sinatra sort of artist, classy and confident. It was immediately evident from the reactions of the people I met that being stylish raised me another notch in the eyes of the executives, who made their approval clear.

Charles was everything I had imagined the head of a record company would be—a charismatic man in a suit and tie, with gray hair and glasses. He was balding and always seemed to have a cigar in hand. Emilio and I met him in his office, then followed him to a conference room with a stunning view of Manhattan sprawling below. There we were joined by other executives and marketing people associated with producing and promoting my album.

Sitting in that room, I began to understand for the first time how the game worked in the music industry. The level of recognition for an artist with a record company started with the head of the company, the main decision maker. It then moved down through the different ranks of people in the company. A meeting like this one, the point of which was to introduce everyone to me and my music, was crucial in launching an album. This kind of meeting confirmed the president's own interest and investment in the artist.

"Jon, we want you to know we're going to use our best efforts to make sure this project is as successful as it can be," Charles said at the outset of the meeting. "You're going to be an important element of this company as a non-format artist breaking through different genres on the charts." Then he asked me to play five or six of the songs from the album for everyone to hear.

Did everyone at that meeting love my music? It was a mixed crowd, and I have no idea if they all loved it or not. What mattered was that the *president* loved my music. I knew that would give me a shot at having a hit album.

By "non-format," Charles meant that the company was going to look at my career and my music—especially "Just Another Day," the single they were about to start marketing to radio stations—as something with a wide appeal. The album had so many different musical influences, they could market it to a broad spectrum of audience types rather than being limited, say, to teenagers who listened solely to pop.

At that time, the only way to market albums and artists was through radio. Today, while the radio is still the main driving force when it comes to connecting audiences with mainstream music, there are dozens of other musical outlets, including downloading and streaming from Pandora or YouTube or any number of other online music sources. Radio promotion takes a lot of marketing dollars and muscle; the advantage of non-format songs like "Just Another Day" was that they could be played on different radio stations across genres.

True to his word, Charles and his team promoted me within every domestic and international outlet through showcase performances and radio. For the musicians in my band who would tour with me, I chose most of the guys I was working with at Emilio's studio, including Miguel. He played keyboard and I wanted him there as cocreator of these songs, even though he'd never intended to tour as a professional musician.

Charles and his team made it clear that I was going to play a big role in promoting my own album. I was happy to take that on, eager to do whatever it took to make that first single—and the whole album—reach as many listeners as possible.

The first place we showcased "Just Another Day" was at the Midem music conference in Cannes, France, where Charles introduced me to EMI's international affiliates. Emilio suggested that Gloria accompany me because she could personally introduce me to the international music community, which in effect was another endorsement. Gloria stepped up to the plate. Moreover, I was flown there on the Concorde. These were all new and exciting moments for me, and every one of them made me feel like I was sleepwalking through a marvelous Technicolor dream. I didn't want to ever wake up!

Having written songs for other artists and worked with them as a vocalist, I knew how tough it was to break into radio stations with a new song. Every now and then I felt a shiver of doubt, thinking, *Holy shit, I might not get anywhere. Then what?*

Then the record label would drop me, that's what.

We started our promotional radio visits in the Northeast. It was like plotting a war campaign. I usually traveled with Adolfo Ordiales, a company executive who is still my best friend and road manager. Our friendship happened naturally, as a result of him remembering me from Miami clubs and then becoming part of Emilio's production crew.

SBK radio promoters strategically pinpointed every radio station they considered a possibility. Systematically, a radio promoter would take Adolfo and me to meet all of the radio executives and DJs at those stations. We'd get in the car at five a.m. and cover five hundred miles a day, visiting different radio stations and trying to persuade them to play my record, then coming back to New York City at the end of the day just to get up and do the whole thing again the next morning. We did that in every corner of every major marketplace where the company wanted to break the single.

Some people liked the record, but others did not. There were program directors at radio stations who would basically tell me to my face, "Look, I'm sorry, 'Just Another Day' is a very nice song, but we'd never play it!"

However, the record company representatives who brought Adolfo and me around to the stations were doggedly persistent. They worked those radio stations with a sledgehammer. Gradually, all of the station managers ended up listening to "Just Another Day"—and liking the song. I thanked God every day for having a company back me so relentlessly, pushing my music.

Little by little, key stations started to come on board and key people started to like the record. One of these was Lee Chesnut at Star 94 in Atlanta. He was a very important program director at that station, which then influenced other stations to play my single.

I was lucky. "Just Another Day" squeaked onto the Top 100 chart at #99 during its debut week. I was still nervous—how easy would it be to fall off the chart, if that's where you started?—but the record executives seemed pleased. The song started creeping upward after two weeks, but the rise was so slow that it kept me awake at night, thinking, *If we don't see results soon, these people are going to drop me any freakin' day.*

At Emilio's insistence, I shot a lush, emotional video for "Just Another Day" on the beach in Miami. This was practically my backyard, but the exotic bilingual culture of Miami and the sensuality of the beach scenes really worked with the song. Emilio wanted to make sure the music video for "Just Another Day" was as sexy as it could be, while at the same time featuring Miami as an international hot spot where things were happening artistically. As if that weren't enough, Gloria even appeared in the video, making a cameo to ensure that it would reach an even wider international audience.

I loved the vibe of that video and trusted Emilio's vision. Even though I lip-synched the song for the video, I gave it my all, trying to connect with the emotional spirit of the song and expressing that emotion through my facial expressions and body language. As always, I was eating up these new experiences and trying to learn everything I could.

SBK had ties to VH1, which was geared more toward adult contemporary music than MTV was, so SBK sent them the music video. VH1 immediately fell in love with it and gave it a lot of airplay. In the 1990s, music videos were hugely important in making the careers of certain artists, so I was pleased to be taken on as a VH1 artist.

In addition to working with Emilio, I now signed on with Jorge Pinos at the William Morris Agency. He represented Gloria and was now going to help book live performances for me. Within five months or so, I was touring internationally and "Just Another Day" continued its steady progress up the charts, finally breaking into the Top 20 and then hitting #10.

No matter where I was, I would get a call from the label every Tuesday to let me know where my single ranked that week. I continually reminded myself that I was lucky to have gotten even this far. As we waited for that weekly call, Adolfo and I would tell each other, "Look, if the song starts dropping right now, it was still a great ride."

At the same time, I'd utter a silent little prayer: *Please don't drop, please don't drop.*

"Just Another Day" got stuck between #12 and #14 for a month or so. At that point, I said to myself, "I'm okay with that," never dreaming that I'd ever reach more listeners with my song than that.

Fate works in funny ways. Baseball is one of Cuba's most beloved sports, and as an overweight kid without an athletic bone in my body, I had longed to be one of those baseball players. Ironically, it was my passion for singing that led me to the playing field.

In 2005, I had the opportunity to play in an All-Star Game with the Hall of Famers. I remember just holding the ball in my hand and marveling that I was there in Detroit, playing in front of a big crowd. My first time up at bat was horrible, but my second time was a moment I'll never forget. It was the bottom of the ninth inning and I was representing the celebrities and Hall of Famers in the American League. There were two outs when I went up to bat and the score was tied. On the life of my children, nobody has any idea how terrifying that was for me. While of course I get anxious before a stage performance, that's nothing compared to how nervous I was at that moment. Even though I knew it was a charity softball game that didn't really mean much, to me it represented my love of the sport.

The crowd was going wild, yet somehow I managed to concentrate—despite how much I had sucked the first time I was up at bat. This time, I zeroed in on the ball, swung the bat, and had a hit, scoring the winning run. At the end of the game, I was voted Most Valuable Player of the game!

Another big baseball-related moment in my career was singing the national anthem in Toronto in 1992. That moment was made even sweeter by the fact that I could now afford to fly my father, who shared my lifelong love of sports, to join me in Toronto.

The 1992 World Series marked the first time that games were ever played outside the United States. That particular game pitted the Toronto Blue Jays against the Atlanta Braves in a beautiful indoor stadium. When it was time for me to sing, I shook off my nerves and became focused on giving the greatest performance I could.

The national anthem is difficult, especially when you sing it a cappella, as I was doing that day. It's a song we all know and respect, yet many great artists blunder through it—especially when the world is watching, the pressure is on, and you definitely don't want to make a mistake. I was excited but terrified. To me, that song represents so much, not only as an artist but as an immigrant to the United States. So many of my wishes and dreams were coming true, largely because my parents had given me the opportunity to become an American citizen and live a free life.

Every time I sing the national anthem, I think about the actual lyrics as I'm singing it. Doing that allows me to focus and go deep in my heart, to a place that really helps my performance be more emotional in a way that connects with the audience. Since that day, I've probably sung the national anthem twenty times for major events, but that day in Toronto was the first and most important time I ever sang it in public.

In Toronto, I sang well, but then I couldn't stay to watch the game because we were headed back to Europe to do more touring! Adolfo and I drove back to the airport as soon as I finished singing. There I got a call informing me that "Just Another Day" had finally hit #10 on the chart.

I figured the song would probably drop from there. Instead, it kept rising, staying in the Top 5 for weeks. I couldn't believe it! After so many hours in the music studio, after all of the days and months and years of uncertainty about my future as a performer, my song was here to stay. And so, I hoped, was I.

While I was touring and promoting my first album in various ways, Emilio was doing some political maneuvers on my behalf behind the scenes. There was no Spanish label at SBK, but after clearing things with them, Emilio used his connections at EMI Latino to present the idea of adapting *Jon Secada* into Spanish. He went full throttle here, pitching me as a crossover artist with major international appeal—especially in the vast Hispanic markets.

The executives didn't even know where I was from at that point. Now that the first album was a success and the timing was right, Emilio met with the record executives at EMI and casually said, "By the way, just so you know, Jon is Cuban. He can sing in

Spanish. Adapting the album wouldn't cost you much, because this guy can do it himself."

Jose Behar at EMI immediately recognized the market potential. He asked Charles if they could have me do a Spanish version of my first album, promising to create their own budget to promote me in the Spanish-language markets. Charles agreed and that's how, just six months after *Jon Secada* debuted, I had a brand-new CD—*Otro Día Más Sin Verte*.

Gloria was instrumental in helping me translate the songs. She had told me earlier, when I was writing the songs for my debut album, that whatever happened to me, "You should always write songs as if you're going to be singing those songs forever, because, God willing, you will sing your songs many, many times."

Now she gave me more good advice as she and another writer from our camp, Stefano, helped me adapt the lyrics of every song on my first album. The important thing about adapting an English song into Spanish, she said, was to "keep the main theme of the song in play. Don't translate anything literally. Just make the song work in Spanish."

Together, we translated the songs in a way that made sure the song's hook was still there, the connection between the emotion in the music and the lyrics that would make the song resonate with listeners and make it difficult to forget. The songs in English were just a starting point for us to write new songs in Spanish, essentially. Once again, I found myself feeling grateful that Gloria and I had both been raised in Miami and could think in two languages.

After translating the songs, I recorded the whole album quickly in the midst of promoting the single and traveling all over the place. On my off days, I would come to Miami to record the songs in Spanish.

Singing in Spanish gave me a different connection to the

music as well, I discovered. My delivery in Spanish was instinctively more passionate, maybe because technically I paid more attention to how I hit the consonants. In addition, the vowel sounds are bigger in Spanish—that's just the nature of the language.

Once the album was completed, Jose Behar ran away with it. For every song I had put out in English, Jose created a single in Spanish, and every song in Spanish was a hit. I began traveling even more, performing not only in Europe and Asia now, but all over Latin America, with an album that connected with audiences. My debut album sold more than six million copies worldwide and was certified triple platinum.

I had been a team player, making the best album I could and promoting it with every ounce of my energy. The results were worth it. I felt blessed, and I counted my blessings in two languages.

CHAPTER TWELVE
Remember Where You Came From

Despite my success in that first year after *Jon Secada* and the quick subsequent release of *Otro Día Más Sin Verte*, I understood the music industry game well enough to know that the record companies were investing money in my career. Any sales I made had to go against the money I'd already been paid by SBK. I had received a generous advance for each album. Nonetheless, the money was just enough to pay for the recording process and touring, with a little bit left over.

When it came time to do my second English CD, the advance from SBK was much larger—a reflection of how well the first one did. The first CD earned millions in sales, so I received a $2.5 million advance on the second album. That was the moment when I understood how much money record companies could make off a successful project.

I tried to look ahead without letting myself worry about what might happen if my second album failed, but that proved to be impossible. Up to this point in time, I had successfully managed my expectations about my career, never dreaming that I'd become a performer on this level. Now, however, I had tasted celebrity and the recognition that comes with it—and the worries.

The minute my music was on the radio, the minute I was in a relationship with this major record label, I was addicted to success. I was now considered one of the best up-and-coming faces in the music industry, and it was both exhilarating and terrifying—even though I hadn't yet reached the pinnacle of what the industry considered "successful." That was still to come, along with heartache.

One morning in Miami, I drove to Emilio's studio and discovered that the 1992 Grammy nominations had just come in. Everyone was excited because my name was on the ballot as one of the nominees for Best Latin Pop Album of the Year and Best New Artist. I couldn't believe it! This was great news not just for me and my career, but for the studio as well.

While everyone at the studio was congratulating me, I felt a wave of gratitude for having been surrounded by such a great team of people at Emilio's studio for the past five years. It never occurred to me that I'd actually *win* the Grammy, since I was going up against some heavy hitters in the industry, including two of my favorite singers, Julio Iglesias and Luis Miguel. It seemed unlikely that my debut album could beat out such established artists. However, just seeing my name on the ballot was a mega thrill.

The Grammy Awards ceremony was held in New York that year. I went with Adolfo to the ceremony and loved every minute of it. There I was, watching people like Billy Ray Cyrus and groups like Arrested Development receiving their awards. I grew up listening to many of the artists I saw that night and I respected them. I recognized what a breakthrough it was for me and my career just to be here.

When my name was announced as the winner of the Best

Latin Pop Album that night, it felt surreal, like an out-of-body experience. I tried hard not to let my thoughts or my ego fly out of control, to just stay grounded in the moment and keep my mind and heart in the right place.

It was difficult to do that. Almost immediately, winning the Grammy translated into more radio airplay for my songs. Between the publishing royalties for the songs I'd written and more bookings for shows, I suddenly started having cash pour into my bank account—more than I'd ever had in my life.

I had spent two years on the road and every one of my singles was on *Billboard*. In Spanish, every song had made it to the Top 5 in Adult Contemporary. Sometime between making my first album and my second, I received my first big royalty check. Sure, I'd gotten money here and there for publishing songs, but nothing like this.

Up to that point, I had been living in the same Hialeah house I'd grown up in with my parents, in the same loft apartment I'd shared with Jo Pat. I was also driving the same car I'd been driving forever, a reliable but definitely well-used Dodge Colt. There was a security guard on the night shift at Emilio's studio whom I'd become friends with over the years. He was a warm, Cuban guy who often talked to me about his car problems.

"Should I get rid of it?" he'd ask me every now and then. "Or should I sink more money into repairs?"

When I got that first big check, I drove to the studio that day and said to the guard, "Listen, bro, you know what? Why don't you take my car?" I handed him the keys, then got a buddy of mine to drive me to a nearby dealership, where I leased the first new car I'd ever had in my life.

Success is a funny thing for entertainers. When you reach a certain level above anything you've hit before, you have no idea what it'll be like until you're living it. You're showered with attention and you have the kind of money you only dreamed of having. The thing about the music industry is that, when you're on top of the game, money flows along like a river and you think it'll never stop.

My mood was dangerously high. The truth—which I discovered almost too late—is that having so much money all at once makes it easy to get caught up in a lifestyle where you're throwing cash around like it's just paper. You get used to having deep pockets and assume life will always be this way. Unfortunately, that isn't true for most of us, artists or not.

I quickly descended into a cycle of dangerous spending. Going out to dinner with the guys in my band after a show, for instance, I'd order $900 bottles of wine. Other times, I'd go on shopping sprees in Las Vegas and drop $15,000 in one shot.

Adolfo was worried about me. Whenever he'd see me order a hugely expensive bottle of wine or something, he'd shake his head and say, "Dude, don't do that. Just chill. Order something less expensive."

It was tough to restrain myself, though. Time and again, I giddily spent money just for the novelty of being able to buy whatever I wanted. It was hard not to indulge when each show was bringing in tens of thousands of dollars and I was regularly receiving royalty checks for hundreds of thousands. Whereas at first I wondered how any of that money could be real, I quickly got addicted to having it. The ready cash was like candy in a pot—I could easily grab another handful whenever I felt like it.

Finally, my parents intervened. "Be very careful how you spend that money, Jon," my father cautioned. "Be sure you protect yourself and prepare for the future."

My parents were proud of my success, but other than telling me how pleased they were about my work with Gloria and my first CD, they never boasted to other people about it. They were still very careful people when it came to spending money or counting on good fortune. They suggested that I invest some of the money that I was earning.

They kept drilling at me until I agreed. I knew they were right. I'd seen too many people in the entertainment business mishandle their finances to the point where they were left with nothing. I forced myself to put the brakes on my spending, other than buying a house on Miami Beach for my parents. The truth is that once you've been poor, you never stop looking over your shoulder. Even though I was enjoying my new wealth and having fun impulsively spending money—and there were times when I spent a lot of money splurging on great meals and hotels and first-class plane tickets—I didn't feel entirely comfortable living that kind of lifestyle. I, too, was always looking over my shoulder, because I couldn't believe this kind of money would keep coming my way.

That's when I realized there was a way to prepare for a future when perhaps I wouldn't have as much money, while also giving back to my parents. They still had their cafeteria and continued to work long hours, running it on their own. They had worked hard all their lives, and although they were still in good health, they were in their sixties. I wanted them to sell the business and relax a little; by taking care of them, I could pay homage to everything they had done for my life and my career.

I had to be crafty about it, though. I knew that if I suggested retirement, my vigorous, stubborn parents would balk at the idea. Instead, I told them I needed their help. "I need you to look after my finances," I said, explaining that with their guidance, I could start saving money instead of spending it. "Please, I want you to sell the cafeteria. You're done with working those long hours. You've been doing that long enough. I want you to help me out and do other things with your time, maybe relax a little."

My father was shocked. "Are you sure?"

"I'm absolutely sure," I said. "Once you sell the business, I'll give you some money for you to invest in some properties for me. Then I'm going to need you to manage those properties, because I'm on the road all the time. Will you do that for me?"

To my delight, my father agreed. They put the cafeteria up for sale and I gave them a chunk of money to invest with free rein to spend it on whatever they saw as a good investment. They did well at it, too. My parents bought several small condominiums around greater Miami and managed the properties for me.

Our history had come full circle. All of the sacrifices my parents had made to leave Cuba, to go to Spain and Costa Rica so they could end up here, providing for me and sending me to college, had paid off. Now I wanted them to reap the fruit from their years of struggling. I felt confident that, no matter what happened, I could make a living as a musician and support them.

By any standards, my career was on a roll. In 1992 I became only the second artist to have two singles on *Billboard*'s HOT 100 for thirty weeks or more with "Just Another Day" and "Do You Believe in Us." I was also the only artist to have four consecutive number one singles from a debut album on *Billboard*'s Latin Singles chart.

Shortly after winning the 1992 Grammy for Best Latin Pop Album, I was also nominated for an American Music Award in the category of Best Adult Contemporary Artist. This award was significant because it was given on the basis of how popular my songs were on the radio.

At this point, it felt almost like my career was on cruise control. Given the success of the first album and my various singles, it was easy now for my agent to book shows and tours. Those, in turn, led to a wave of fresh opportunities as I met more people in the entertainment business.

I had become enough of a celebrity that I was now recognized almost anywhere I went, and I enjoyed having fans. While other music celebrities were mobbed, I was lucky; my fans were a good mix of mostly adult men and women who were genuinely appreciative of my music and respectful toward me as a person.

The brand-new experiences hurtling my way included television shows. Gradually I started doing more and more regional television shows. Then came the first big media break: Joan Rivers invited me to appear on her TV show, and I found out for the first time what national exposure could do for my career.

The Tonight Show asked me to do an appearance soon after that. This was a major coup; generally, you couldn't get on that show until your song broke the Top 20, and mine did that just as Jay Leno was taking over from Johnny Carson. I was extremely nervous doing *The Tonight Show* for the first time, since I knew how hard the record company had been working to get me opportunities to perform at a national level.

Before I went on the show, I said a little prayer that went something like this: "Please, please don't let me screw anything up tonight. At least let me *look* relaxed even if I'm not!"

For most of the big national television shows, I would always go through a pre-telecast interview with one of the show's producers. *The Tonight Show* was no exception.

"We're going to ask you some questions about yourself," the producer said, "and then Jay will pick from some of these questions when you get on the air. Do you have anything interesting that's happened that would make a good story tonight?"

As she started grilling me about my past, I suddenly thought of Don Johnson. "Don Johnson owes me money," I said.

The minute the words were out of my mouth, the producer pounced on them. "Perfect!" she said. "That's going to be great on air."

What had I done? I couldn't believe I'd said that! I tried to comfort myself by saying that Jay probably wouldn't have time to ask me about Don Johnson; often there wasn't much time for the interview after I performed.

I put my worries aside. As always when I was nervous, I went into hyper-concentration mode. I performed well that night despite my jitters.

The minute Jay and I were talking, though, the first question out of his mouth was, "So is it true Don Johnson owes you money?"

To heck with it, I thought. *I'm going to tell the truth.* Who knew? Maybe Don Johnson would hear this on the air and pay me. "Yeah, he owes me money," I said, and told him the story.

Years later, I saw Don at one of Emilio's parties. As we approached each other, I gave him a cordial look and said, "Hey, how you doing?"

Don nodded back but kept walking past me. Obviously, he didn't appreciate what I'd done. But he didn't pay me back, either.

Although I didn't fully realize it at the time, I was a pioneer in the music industry in the early 1990s. Unlike most Latin artists who had managed to cross over into the Anglo market after first establishing themselves with Spanish-language albums, I represented the first of a new breed: a Latin artist who signed as an Anglo act first, before creating a hit album in Spanish.

What happened with me was just a foreshadowing of what's happening today in pop music, with so many artists in mainstream music coming from different ethnic and musical backgrounds but making it in the Anglo market. I'm proud of all of my friends and colleagues who helped pave the way for crossover artists making it on the scene today—and of my own small part in that. I'm also happy that I was able to look after my parents and show my appreciation for everything they'd done for me. I hope to never forget where I came from, or the people who helped me along the road to success.

CHAPTER THIRTEEN
Celebrity Is Like Crack

With the success of "Just Another Day," my expectations—and my life—changed overnight. I'd had a taste of success and wanted more. The game was different now. Instead of being completely happy to take whatever came my way as a working musician in Miami, I had reached a new level as an entertainer. I was eager to keep proving to SBK, and to myself, that my career as a pop singer was going to continue growing.

By early fall of 1993, I'd turned my attention to working with Miguel Morejon on the second CD, *Heart, Soul, and a Voice*. The first song we wrote was called "If You Go." We had another couple of songs left over that didn't make it onto *Jon Secada*, including "Mental Picture," but we needed to write some more. It felt great to go back to the drawing board and start creating again.

Besides working with Miguel, I also wrote songs with the production team at Emilio's studio, which had really grown a lot since our early days together. I was nervous about producing this sophomore CD, because I knew the people at SBK were once again investing heavily in me as an artist.

"Let's try to come up with something that sounds like 'Just Another Day,'" I said to Miguel. "Maybe if we do a follow-up to that song, it can be the stepping-stone for the success of this second CD."

At the same time, it was my instinct as a musician to experiment by integrating different influences into my songwriting. I wanted this CD to have a harder, more urban sound, so a lot of the arrangements and drumbeats were more aggressive in some of the songs, while others were more like the songs on *Jon Secada*.

Once we completed *Heart, Soul, and a Voice*, I wanted the first single released to be "Whipped." That song was different for me. It was a very hard-edged pop, rock, rhythm-and-blues fusion song. I loved it because I felt like it really represented the best of the new kind of sound I was producing. I had the support of SBK's second-in-command, Daniel Glass, to release that as the first single.

Then one day I was doing a photo session when Charles Koppelman called me directly. "Jon, please don't do this," he said. "You know the company is going to support you a million percent. But don't deviate. Don't let your fans or radio down with such a departure."

His reasoning was simple: the song "If You Go," which I'd written with Miguel, had more of the flavor, essence, sound, and feeling of the songs on *Jon Secada*, and that album had struck a chord with many people—an audience that would likely want to hear (and buy) more of the same kind of songs from me. "Go with the song that people are going to identify you with," Charles urged.

I was resistant at first. Wasn't I an artist? And shouldn't every artist be willing to take risks? Plus, wasn't this the high point of my career—a time when it was not only possible, but a good idea for me to strut my versatility as a singer and songwriter?

On the other hand, I was impressed that Charles had called me directly, and I was—as always—a team player. SBK had invested money, loyalty, and hard work in my career, and if anyone knew how to market music, it was Charles Koppelman. I agreed to make "If You Go" the first single.

Charles was spot-on. That single quickly turned out to be a Top 10 hit and another Top 5 in Adult Contemporary. In 1993, I was named Best Male Vocalist in a *Rolling Stone* poll and one of the ten "sexiest male rock stars" by *Playgirl*. *Otra Día Más Sin Verte* earned Best Latin Pop Album of the Year at the *Billboard* Latin Music Awards, and I also earned the title of Best New Latin Pop Artist that year.

In keeping with this edgier new sound on the second CD, Emilio and others on my team wanted me to have a cooler look and lifestyle. "Look, Jon," they said, "you're doing all of this very edgy, sexy music, so you need to look and act like that kind of guy. We need to spice up your image."

Deep down, I was a creature of habit. I had hunkered down in my Miami Beach home and was still trying to recover from my divorce. I continued to see my parents often. However, I wanted to show respect for the management team and the record company, so I let them dictate my new image and tried to have fun with the process.

My image makeover began with the record company renting a separate house in Miami Beach for me, where I was expected to give a lot of parties in my beach house as part of the promotional junket for *Heart, Soul, and a Voice*. Part of me—the musician part— always wanted to just go hang out with the guys in whatever band was playing at those parties instead of playing the celebrity, since that was the habit I'd had for so many years—but I knew I had to play a different part for the moment.

Next, my management team hired Ingrid Casares, a close friend of Madonna's, to help spice up my image. She was wonderful to work with, and in her own right she had a tremendous network of celebrities she was representing. The first thing Ingrid did was help me dress in a hipper, more fashion-conscious way. I was also sent into social situations so that I'd be seen mingling with celebrities.

The first video for the CD, for the song "If You Go," was tremendous; the director came up with a wonderful story line and we shot it outside of Los Angeles. The director and set designer deliberately made everything—including me—look rugged but with a sensual edge.

All of this was being done to create an image of someone I was not. On the inside I was not a cool guy. I was still organized and a little anxious, the kind of nice guy who is always on time and builds relationships with other people rather than burning bridges when things don't go my way. But I understood that to market my new album successfully, I'd have to be perceived as an outgoing, sexy single guy who is seen with celebrities and dating hot girls.

These dates were setups. Models or other entertainers would show up with me at certain events just so we'd have our pictures taken and sent to magazines. One memorable evening, for instance, Toni Braxton's manager called to ask if I could accompany her to the American Music Awards; she'd been nominated and needed a date.

I flew to Los Angeles and pulled up to her hotel in a limo. When I knocked on the door of her suite, her parents were there and Toni was still getting ready. I talked with her parents for a while and then the two of us headed out together.

Of course, showing up together at the American Music Awards created a buzz, just as both of our management teams had intended. The minute we stepped out of the limo, Toni took my hand for the walk up the red carpet. The surprise element of us appearing as a couple caused such a media frenzy that we were swarmed by cameras and couldn't walk until the security people parted the crowd. Toni gave me a kiss as we were sitting down, and the next day our photos were all over the newspapers and television talk shows.

We went out a few more times after that. There was definitely an attraction between us. Toni is a lovely lady and a major talent. However, as beautiful as she was, and as fun as it was to share the spotlight with her for a while, I realized at that point in my life that I couldn't be with a woman whose lifestyle and ambition were so similar to mine. It was frankly a scary thought, knowing that both of us were under the same demands from our schedules and always in the media spotlight. If I married another celebrity, there would never be any type of normalcy in my life, because we'd both be traveling and there would be no home life at the end of a tour, or even at the end of the day.

My parents had always talked about wanting grandchildren, but they were supportive about my divorce from Jo Pat, knowing that it was ultimately for the best, and they didn't seem to mind that I was in my thirties now, but nowhere close to being ready to have a family. This was the first time I'd lived away from home for any length of time. But that was fine. I was traveling so much that home was just a bed to me and little more.

"Don't you dare think about getting married again," my father cautioned me, because he saw my behavior with women. Although I wasn't exactly a party animal, music is a great aphrodisiac, and I was finding it easy to meet women now that I was better known as an entertainer. "You shouldn't get married in the position you're in," he said. "You went through all of this hardship and emotional stress to get divorced. Now it's time to discover yourself. Allow yourself some freedom, *mi hijo*."

My friends, too, warned me about getting involved with any one woman in particular. "You're on the road all the time, man," they said. "It'll never work out."

But did I listen? Although I was dating many women and enjoying it, there was a side of me that still wanted to be attached to one person.

It was around this time that I became involved with Ana, a woman I'd met when I was teaching at Miami Dade College and at the University of Miami, where she took one of my ensemble classes when I was a graduate student. Ana was half Cuban and a talented singer. I liked her immediately and respected her as a singer.

One thing led to another. As I started booking more shows, I hired Ana to sing background vocals. That snowballed into us clicking on a more intimate level as we traveled together, and we began dating.

I was unfair and unfaithful to Ana almost from day one. As much as I cared deeply for her, I knew at once that I'd made a mistake by getting involved and letting her think I felt as strongly about her as she did about me. I should have been smarter and not let us get that close. But once again I found myself shying away from being honest, because I dreaded the confrontation.

Things were even more complicated because we worked and socialized together so often, yet I somehow managed to find plenty of time and opportunities to cheat on Ana while we were touring. I felt immensely guilty every time. Yet I couldn't seem to stop myself.

Finally, in the hope of resolving my issues and resurrecting the relationship between Ana and me, I decided to invite her to go on a trip to Spain with me and my parents. It was a little bit of a promotional gig, but it was mostly a vacation; I hoped that Ana and I would get closer, and that being with my parents would remind me of all that I wanted in a woman and in a marriage.

It should have worked. Ana spoke Spanish, so there wasn't the same language divide between her and my parents that Samantha and Jo Pat had experienced. However, my mother picked up right away on the fact that this was a troubled relationship and I wanted my freedom. She also knew me well enough—better than I knew myself, sometimes—to see that this relationship was going nowhere. In every gesture and glance toward me, my mother was communicating that she thought I should get my act together instead of stringing this poor girl along.

It wasn't a disastrous trip, but it wasn't always a comfortable one, and by the end of it I knew that there was no future with me for Ana. However, it wasn't until we flew home from Spain and I finished my first tour that we actually stopped seeing each other completely, and even then, we only broke up because Ana was brave enough to do it. "I'm out of here," she declared. "This is so not for me."

Clearly, I wasn't ready to enter into a serious relationship with another woman so soon after my divorce. At the same time, I wanted to be the sort of man who could be in a loving, committed relationship. The breakup with Ana left me feeling not only sad because I'd hurt her, but also depressed and confused about how I had managed to reach a point in my life where I was surrounded by people, yet couldn't seem to be truly intimate with a woman emotionally as well as physically. Instead of being honest, I was devious.

I couldn't let myself get involved and hurt another good woman like that. My father was right. I needed to be alone. And so I spent the next months working, traveling, and knowing I was lucky to be in this position as an entertainer, but at the same time feeling incredibly lonely. I was in a boot camp of self-discovery, as I vowed to fix whatever I needed to fix and get to know myself better before embarking on another serious relationship.

As I promoted my second album, I earned an endorsement from AT&T. The company wanted me to participate in the Spanish-speaking version of the TrueVoice campaign that Whitney

Houston had done in the Anglo market. I was walking on air when my agent delivered the news. Appearing in the AT&T campaign would give me a tremendous touring budget as well as a lot of national exposure.

For the commercial, AT&T flew me over the Grand Canyon in a helicopter, where I was taken to the top of a huge cliff. I stood on top of the cliff, opened my arms as if embracing the view, and sang my heart out, wearing a holster to secure me to the rock face. I loved every minute of it.

The tour itself was equally amazing. With that one sponsor, I had a bigger budget and could extend my touring, reaching a much wider audience.

SBK was still doing everything in its power to support the heck out of "If You Go" as the first single. Meanwhile I recruited the help of Madonna's younger brother, Chris Ciccone, who had designed the stage for Madonna's 1990 Blond Ambition Tour and directed her Girlie Show World Tour in 1993, to help me produce the tour for *Heart, Soul, and a Voice*. Chris had a keen eye for stage management and design, and this time I wanted to stage a show that was more like a theatrical piece along the lines of what Madonna was doing for her shows, though on a smaller scale.

Chris designed the look of the tour, creating a lot of the initial production elements, from the wardrobe to the show itself. We really plotted out how the songs flowed from one to the next, the costume changes, and how different musical interludes could create the moods we wanted.

Although I wasn't a dancer, we added a lot of choreography, so that the background singers and I could produce a lot of movement onstage to keep the audience riveted. This was a huge growing experience for me as a recording artist on a different level, and an important step to take, because I really wanted to become more of an all-around entertainer, not just a singer.

The tour, which launched in 1994 and took us all over the

United States and Latin America, involved some fun mixing and matching of songs from both of my albums. The set list was high energy between the ballads, and we got lucky: there were no disasters on the road and we all had a great time.

Of all of the places we played, my favorite was Radio City Music Hall, where I did three sold-out nights in a row. Looking out at all of those people who'd come to see me was awe-inspiring. I had a heightened sense of responsibility during that tour, of course, since it was up to me to make it a success, but having traveled with Gloria, I'd had good training. Walking onto that Radio City Music Hall stage, I realized I was living my dream. I couldn't imagine ever giving up the lifestyle I'd managed to create for myself.

Throughout my career, I have tried to always stay calm and controlled even during crises. However, as I began experiencing a celebrity lifestyle for the first time, there were a few times when I found myself pushed beyond my patience as I came under the wrong kind of media scrutiny.

Once, for example, a reporter wrote an article claiming that I was a Castro supporter. All of the information in the article was completely untrue, but very detailed when it came to things I had allegedly said. I was in Venezuela when the piece appeared; I called Emilio's office as soon as I read the damning piece.

"I want you to do something about this reporter!" I shouted. "I want to strangle him!" I used every foul word in the book.

Yes, I was an Afro-American Cuban whose father had been jailed by Castro and whose family had given up everything to be free. I worked hard for whatever opportunities I earned as an entertainer—and as an immigrant to the United States—and I would continue to work for whatever came my way. These had been non-issues in my career.

However, being called a Castro supporter after all my family had gone through wasn't just a sensitive issue for me: it was the worst insult anyone could hurl my way. "You know my father was put in prison during Castro's regime, right?" I yelled all the way from Venezuela to Miami. "We need to fix this!"

In the end, we had to hire an attorney, because the reporter kept insisting that he'd recorded a conversation in which I'd expressed my Castro sympathies. I couldn't believe he'd go that far out on a limb. Maybe the guy actually believed that I would get confused about what I had said. Finally, though, the reporter backed down when we legally forced him to produce the tape and there was nothing on it. He still didn't apologize, but he at least revised his story.

There was another incident, too, with a woman somewhere in the Northeast. As I was promoting my second CD, this woman started sending faxes to radio and TV stations with a fabricated story about me being involved with a sixteen-year-old girl and fathering a child with her. This woman cited detailed information about people associated with my career.

At one point, I got a call from a well-known celebrity with Univision, Raúl de Molina. I thanked him for actually calling me and at least hearing my side of the story: that there was absolutely no truth in those faxes from this woman.

Emilio, who had some influence with Raúl, was present during the phone call. He told him this was a completely fabricated story with no validity whatsoever, and he never reported it on television. Nonetheless, the situation continued for a year. Once again I had to hire private investigators and an attorney to track down this person. It took a while to find her, and for her to stop sending these weird fictional stories. She never apologized or admitted any wrongdoing.

One side effect of being a celebrity, as I was discovering, is that you are in the public eye. Any time you walk out of your house, you're completely exposed and vulnerable to the people out there who are going to try to take you down. You have to be alert, but take things in stride.

I continued going out with various women for the next six months as part of promoting *Heart, Soul, and a Voice*, meeting people like Madonna and k.d. lang and having these out-of-body experiences in fantastic party situations I never could have imagined being in. Madonna had a house out on Star Island at that time, and she was already an icon in the music industry. I admired her music, and was pleased to find that she was very grounded, very real, talking about everything from sex to sports.

We hung out at her house for a while, then went out to a basketball game. Afterward, Madonna said, "You know what? I've always wanted to get my belly button pierced."

With the noisy urging of friends egging her on, Madonna went to a tattoo parlor in the middle of Miami Beach, with all of us in tow, to spontaneously have her navel pierced.

I say "spontaneously," but I wondered afterward whether it really was. Madonna was intelligent and quick-witted. She was also extremely careful, very in tune with how she presented herself. She was fun to be around, and definitely an entertainer who was daringly on the edge, but she was always very controlled. I admired and appreciated the fact that Madonna knew how to party and speak her mind, while always being conscious of what kind of impact she was making. Whatever she did, she did deliberately, and with care. I hoped to be the same way.

I had many opportunities to grow as an entertainer during that time. One highlight of my career was performing "Angel" in a public ceremony for Pope John Paul II. The concert was held in Central Park, with more than half a million people attending. It was a surreal moment, seeing the pontiff sitting there and knowing he was listening to me sing.

I also visited the White House many times, and President

George W. Bush appointed me to serve on the President's Advisory Commission on Educational Excellence for Hispanics.

Of all of these trips to Washington, D.C., however, the most memorable was for President Bill Clinton's inauguration, where I had the honor of belting out Ben E. King's classic song "Stand by Me" with Luther Vandross, Melissa Etheridge, Shai, and Ben himself. The day was so cold that we were all wrapped in scarves and topcoats, but I didn't care.

Before we went onstage to perform, we were corralled in a tent area. I didn't mind how long I waited, because I was in a place that was a virtual traffic jam of celebrities. I'm sure my jaw was practically dropping to the floor as I walked around, astonished to be included among them.

At one point, I was standing next to Jack Nicholson as he was watching somebody speak on the monitor. He grunted and glanced at me over his shoulder. "What a nice speaking voice," he said.

"Yeah, you're right," I agreed. That was all I could manage. But still, I'd been spoken to by Jack Nicholson, and that was enough for me. There weren't a lot of Latinos asked to be part of the inaugural, and I was just taking it all in, feeling blessed to be there and represent Hispanic Americans. If this was the celebrity life, then I was definitely addicted to it.

CHAPTER FOURTEEN
Family Is Everything

For the purposes of publicity, it was important for me to be seen as social, single, and available, so my management team continued to set me up with different women. The best thing to happen to me during the whirlwind social year when I was promoting *Heart, Soul, and a Voice* was the date that led me to Maritere Vilar, the woman who would eventually become my second wife, and who is still my partner in life.

I met Mari in the same way I was meeting so many women during that time: through a blind date set up by a mutual acquaintance in the studio. He said, "Hey, Jon, listen, now that you're getting out some, take a look at this picture of a girl I know. What do you think?"

The girl in the picture wasn't just pretty. She was gorgeous: a dark-haired, leggy dancer who had helped choreograph a couple of videos for Estefan Enterprises. "She's cute," I commented.

"Yeah?" this guy said. "Great. Why don't you ask this girl out?"

"Sure," I replied. "Set us up."

My first date with Mari was to a Janet Jackson concert. She was somewhat tricked into the date when our mutual friend called her to say, "Hey, are you willing to go to a Janet Jackson concert? Jon Secada's going to go with some other people from the Estefan studio, so we're inviting you to come along."

Mari said yes, unaware of the fact that "we" meant "I" was going to show up at her house as her date. She was completely taken aback when I arrived, alone and in a limo, to pick her up for the concert—she had been under the impression that it was going to be a group outing. We started to chitchat as we drove to the concert, and as we arrived, I had to ask her a favor.

"Look, I know this is going to seem weird, but can you just hold my hand as we walk into the concert?" I said.

Mari laughed and said, "Okay, sure. I can do that."

I was struck right away by how pretty Mari was, of course, but I was also attracted to her lively, bright spirit. We clicked on a number of levels, not least because her background was similar to mine: she was born in the United States, but to a Cuban family, and she still lived at home with her parents and enjoyed spending time with her large, noisy extended family.

Mari had been raised by conservative Catholic parents rooted in Latin traditions. She'd led a sheltered life, unlike many of the other women I'd been dating, and I was immediately in tune with her Cuban American values. We enjoyed the same music and the same foods, and we expressed ourselves in very similar ways. Mari wasn't an entertainer, but she was a dancer and appreciative of the arts. I'd never met anyone like her and felt immediately and powerfully drawn to her.

At that time, however, I was officially still seeing Ana. This was just a publicity date, like any other. Or at least that's what I told myself. I didn't connect the dots between how much I enjoyed this woman's company and the fact that someday a real love could blossom between us.

I knew I had a half sister, Diosdada Secada, who was thirteen years older than I was, but I hadn't ever spent any significant time with her as a child in Cuba. I hadn't seen or heard from her since leaving the island. Diosdada had been estranged from my father for reasons I never understood, but always assumed had something to do with my father's divorce from his first wife.

It was only after my half brother, Francisco, died in the mid-eighties that Diosdada and my father began to repair their relationship by letter. In 1994, Diosdada began writing to him about her desire to immigrate to the United States.

"I'm ready to leave Cuba if I can," she said. "I've become disappointed and frustrated with living here."

What's more, she wanted to bring one of her two daughters—my niece, who was then nineteen years old—with her. The other daughter was married and settled in Cuba.

This conversation had taken place while I was touring. When I returned to Miami, I went to my parents' house for dinner as usual, and my father talked to me about it. "Look," he said, "Diosdada is saying that she wants to come to the States, but she's afraid she wouldn't be welcome here and shouldn't do that."

It was because of me, my father explained, that Diosdada was hesitant. She was afraid that I would resent her for asking. She still felt guilty for having avoided getting to know me when I was a child, and now it would be up to me to help sort out the paperwork, sponsor her, and pay to get my half sister and niece settled in Florida. She was afraid it was too much to ask.

It wasn't. I knew how much Diosdada meant to my father. Besides, to our small family, any family at all was a wonderful thing. "That's ludicrous for her to be worried about me," I said. "If she wants to come here, let's make it happen."

I wrote my sister a letter the very next day, saying that whatever family issues had transpired in the past, they were in the past. "We're family," I said. "If you're comfortable with this arrangement, I want you to let me take care of you. At the end of the day, I want you here. Let's do this."

I handled the paperwork, filing an official claim for Diosdada and her daughter, Lori, to emigrate to the United States as political refugees from Cuba. I was still traveling all over the place between the United States and Latin America for the next six months. By the time I returned to Miami, she and Lori had made it to this country.

I pulled up to my parents' house in Miami Beach. They knew I was coming; Diosdada was standing out in the driveway with Lori to greet me. It was a little strange, but we hugged like nothing had ever happened, laughing and crying a little, too, and I knew I'd done the right thing.

My niece started going to school immediately and became a beautician in a salon. Eventually, Diosdada's other daughter came to Miami as well. Diosdada held different jobs and then stayed home to take care of her grandchildren. Meanwhile, I helped support them, finding them a place to live and giving them money until they were able to support themselves.

Somewhat to my surprise, my mother was every bit as welcoming as I was. She was a great support to my half sister and nieces, and when my father's first wife came, my mother welcomed her as well. Enough years had passed that there were no hard feelings between them. Now I, too, had a big crowd for holiday dinners and birthdays and weekend parties. Time really does have a way of healing life's hurts.

Occasionally, I would see my father sitting in the living room with his two wives and still feel amused by the whole thing, especially when he was silently observing my mother and his ex-wife chatting amiably over the grandchildren. It might look a little dysfunctional to outsiders. To me, though, watching my parents embrace these people after so much had happened and having my sister here reconfirmed for me that family is everything, no matter what shape it comes in.

CHAPTER FIFTEEN
All the World's a Stage to Learn On

As my touring was winding down in 1995, I got a call from my agent, Jorge Pinos, explaining that a producer might be interested in having me do a Broadway show.

"Broadway?" I exclaimed, puzzled. "Why would someone ask me to be in a Broadway show?"

Jorge explained that Broadway shows were beginning to ask celebrities to headline their productions as an additional draw for audiences. "It's a new trend where Broadway producers call on certain artists because their name can give their shows additional stature," he said. "If you want to do it, there's a lot of money to be made, but of course it'll be a lot of work, too. Are you interested?"

I was intrigued by the offer. In high school I had done musical theater, and in college I'd had roles in musical revues and even in an operetta. I'd always been curious about acting, too, and what better platform could there be for me to try out my acting chops than a Broadway production? So I said yes.

The call from New York came at the perfect time. Our tour had just ended and my second album had gone platinum, so I had some downtime. The producers only wanted me to commit for six months.

The show, it turned out, was *Grease*. The producers wanted me not only to take on one of the roles, but to perform the leading role of Danny Zuko. I was thrilled to be cast in such a large part, particularly since I would be among the first Latinos to really have a kind of presence at that level on the Broadway stage.

I was also terrified. I knew the producers were going to promote the heck out of me taking on that role, so I'd better do it well.

The producers set me up in an apartment in Trump Tower. We only had two weeks to rehearse with me in the part of Danny. "How in the world am I going to learn all of this in two weeks?" I wondered as I ran through the songs for the first time and realized that my presence in the show was nearly constant, whether it was for singing, dance numbers, or other scenes.

The answer? A rigorous rehearsal schedule and a stage manager who was determined to drill me on the songs and dance routines. The producers were going to make sure I was as prepared as possible before I appeared in New York City.

I had a lot of lyrics and music to learn, but the singing didn't worry me as much as the dancing. *Grease* had complicated staging and the dance numbers were extremely challenging, especially the three or four high school dance numbers. I went to see the show several times as part of my preparation, but even then, it was difficult for me to envision myself in the role of Danny. There was one particular number that dealt with a tire routine, and at the end of the show there was also a big dance number I'd have to pull off while getting through some tongue-twisting doo-wop lyrics. On top of that, I wanted to do a good job as an actor.

Before having me appear on Broadway, the producers wanted

to make sure I'd mastered the part, so we did a week in Michigan and a week in Hawaii before opening in New York. Once again, I took on this job with all of the energy and focus I brought to every assignment, and it was fun playing my role as I started to understand the dances and the songs. At the end of the two weeks, when I did step into the role of Danny on Broadway, I was pretty good. That gave me the confidence to have fun with the part.

The Broadway cast of *Grease* was made up of seasoned, extremely talented entertainers who all had previous Broadway experience. I was so appreciative of the way they included me and helped me out whenever I needed it. I think they understood how much I respected them and wanted to be a part of the ensemble. Inhabiting another person was really difficult, and I wanted to do it as well as possible. I made a point of asking the stage manager and director for critiques and appreciated all of the notes they gave me. I knew that was the only way I could improve as an actor.

It wasn't until I'd actually performed in a Broadway role that I realized how naive I'd been about the high level of stamina and talent it takes to be a stage entertainer of that caliber. We did eight shows a week; it was impossible not to feel torn up in the process of playing that many shows back to back. Plus, just living alone in New York City was an experience in itself. The show spanned the winter months, and I had never lived anyplace that actually had snow and ice.

In retrospect, I should have taken it easy, given what happened during that Broadway stint, but at the time I thought I was nearly invincible. Yes, I was on Broadway, I thought, but so what? I couldn't just freeze my songwriting career for one show, even if that show was *Grease* with me in the leading role!

No, I wanted to continue writing songs and further make my mark as a singer at the same time. I was such a rookie Broadway entertainer that I had no idea what kind of energy I'd need to get through those shows. I just proceeded to live my usual manic life around them.

One of the first things I did when I arrived in New York was to set up a recording studio in my apartment. Next, I talked my friend Miguel into moving to New York for six months so that he and I could keep writing songs together.

Other friends were coming and going from my apartment, too, and we'd be working together or going out right up until curtain call every night. After each show I'd go out for drinks with friends or the other entertainers in the show. In the morning, I'd do interviews or other promotional things associated with my career, then write songs and work on demos, just as I'd been doing back home. I even moved my parents to New York. In other words, I created my own little Miami life in New York, but with one big difference: I added a Broadway show to my schedule. The weekends were especially murderous, with two shows on Saturday and two more on Sunday.

It was during this time that EMI knocked on my door and I made a deal with them to produce an all-Spanish CD. We actually finished writing the songs, completed preproduction, and recorded my third album, *Amor*, while I was performing on Broadway. We even made a music video to accompany the release of the album.

I was pleased by the album. Slowly but surely, however, my hectic schedule began to take its toll. My voice started getting huskier. I was singing as well as I could, but then something happened to me that had never happened before. It was one of the scariest times of my life.

With just a month left of my first stint on Broadway, I started one particular performance with my voice feeling strained. As I was singing and dancing and doing everything else associated with my role, by the middle of the first act, I knew I was in trouble.

My dad and me across the
street from our apartment
in Havana, Cuba. *(top left)* \
Mi papá y yo al otro lado de
la calle donde estaba nuestro
departamento en La Habana,
Cuba *(arriba a la izquierda)*.

With my parents at a park in
Havana. *(top right)* \ Con mis
papás en un parque en La
Habana *(arriba a la derecha)*.

Sporting a baseball outfit in
the hallway of our Havana
apartment building. *(left)* \
Vestido como beisbolista
en el pasillo de nuestro
departamento en La Habana
(izquierda).

All photos courtesy of the author unless otherwise noted. / Todas las fotografías son cortesía del
autor salvo que se indique lo contrario.

Waiting to take down a piñata at one of my birthday parties in Havana. \ Esperando mi turno para romper la piñata durante una de mis fiestas de cumpleaños en La Habana.

An official elementary school class picture. \ Una fotografía oficial de la escuela primaria.

My family arriving in Costa Rica in 1972. \ Mi familia llegando a Costa Rica en 1972.

Taking first communion next to my mother while we still lived in Spain. \ Haciendo mi primera comunión junto a mi madre cuando todavía vivíamos en España.

With Elvy Rose Alvarez during dress rehearsal of my very first musical in high school. \ Con Elvy Rose Álvarez durante el ensayo de vestuario de mi primera obra musical de la secundaria.

My prom photo. \ Mi fotografía del baile de fin de cursos.

Me during Tae Kwon Do class. *(top left)* \ Yo, durante una clase de Tae Kwon Do *(arriba a la izquierda)*.

My parents, our dear friend Lizama, and me in our cafeteria in Miami. *(bottom left)* \ Mis papás, nuestra querida amiga Lizama y yo en nuestra cafetería de Miami *(abajo a la izquierda)*.

Me in Japan during my tour with Takanaka. *(bottom right)* \ Yo en Japón durante mi gira con Takanaka *(abajo a la derecha)*.

With Larry Lapin, my mentor from University of Miami School of Music. \ Con Larry Lapin, mi mentor de la escuela de Música de la Universidad de Miami.

Singing with the Company in Miami. \ Cantando con la Compañía en Miami.

With Emilio Estefan at a music industry party. \ Con Emilio Estefan en una fiesta de la industria de la música.

Jogging on the beach with Emilio in Acapulco, Mexico. *(top)* \ Trotando en la playa con Emilio, en Acapulco, México *(arriba)*.

While on tour with Gloria Estefan, I had the chance to revisit the cafeteria my parents owned in Costa Rica. *(middle)* \ Durante nuestra gira con Gloria Estefan tuve la oportunidad de volver a la cafetería que fue propiedad de mis papás en Costa Rica *(en medio)*.

Signing my first record contract with SBK / EMI. *(bottom)*\ Firmando mi primer contrato de grabación con SBK /EMI *(abajo)*.

With my castmates from *Grease*. \ Con mis compañeros del elenco de *Grease*.

Filming an AT&T commercial in the canyons of Utah. \ Filmando un comercial de AT&T en los cañones de Utah.

At Super Bowl XXVI with Gloria and Emilio Estefan in 1992. \ En 1992, durante el Super Bowl XXVI, con Gloria y Emilio Estefan.

Hanging out with my father during one of my promotional tours in 1993. \ Con mi padre durante una de mis giras de promoción en 1993.

With the great Luciano Pavarotti in 1996. \ Con el gran Luciano Pavarotti en 1996.

With Mari and her parents on her twenty-fourth birthday—the day they finally accepted us as a couple! \ Con Mari y sus papás en su cumpleaños número veinticuatro, ¡el mismo día en que finalmente nos aceptaron como pareja!

On a summer trip to Disney with Mari during our engagement. \ Con Mari, en un viaje de verano a Disney cuando éramos novios.

Mari and me during our wedding ceremony. \ Mari y yo durante nuestra boda.

Everyone doing the Macarena at our wedding. \ Todos bailando la Macarena durante la boda.

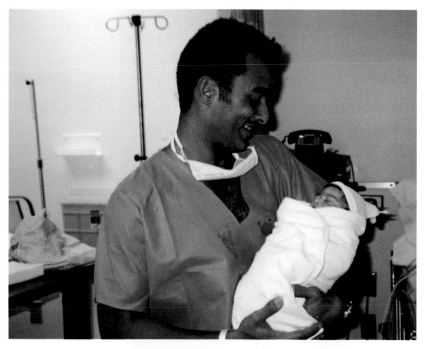

February 15, 1999, the day Mikaela was born. \ 15 de febrero de 1999: el día en que nació Mikaela.

Jon Henri's baptism in November 2002. Gloria and Emilio are his godparents. \ El bautizo de Jon Henri en noviembre de 2002. Gloria y Emilio son sus padrinos.

My fortieth birthday party at Bongos. \ Celebrando mis cuarenta años en Bongos.

My father with Mikaela. \ Mi padre con Mikaela.

Singing onstage with the kids during a concert in Miami in 2004. \ Cantando en el escenario con mis hijos durante un concierto en Miami en 2004.

With my father on my parents' fiftieth wedding anniversary. \ Con mi padre el día de las Bodas de Oro de mis papás.

With my parents on my forty-fourth birthday.\ Con mis papás celebrando mis cuarenta y cuatro años.

Me in full makeup for *Cabaret*. \ Yo, completamente maquillado para *Cabaret*.

On the set of *Latin American Idol* with Jon Henri. \ Con Jon Henri en el set de *Latin American Idol*.

A poster for *Latin American Idol*: (*left to right*) Gustavo Sanchez, Erika de la Vega, me, Mimi Hernandez, and Monchi Balestra. \ Un póster para *Latin American Idol*. De izquierda a derecha: Gustavo Sánchez, Erika de la Vega, yo, Mimi Hernández, y Monchi Balestra.

A family photo taken at Mika's sixth birthday party. \ La familia con Mika en su fiesta de cumpleaños número seis.

Taking a break with the kids during the photo shoot for my album *A Christmas Fiesta*. \ Descansando con los niños durante la sesión fotográfica de mi álbum *A Christmas Fiesta*.

Performing at the 2007 LARAS/ MusiCares ceremony. \ Cantando en la ceremonia MusiCares de los LARAS 2007.

Behind the scenes from my *Classics* album photo shoot. \ Detrás de las cámaras en la sesión fotográfica de mi álbum *Classics*.

Performing in Turkey. *(left)* \ Cantando en Turquía *(izquierda)*.

A picture with my band in Turkey: (*left to right*) Jon Rose, Jack Ciano, me, Javier Carrion, Lindsey Blair. \ Una fotografía con mi banda en Turquía. De izquierda a derecha: Jon Rose, Jack Ciano, yo, Javier Carrión, Lindsey Blair.

Performing at the 2007 ABC Christmas Parade with the *Dancing with the Stars* cast. \ Cantando en el Desfile Navideño de ABC de 2007 con el elenco de *Dancing with the Stars*.

Family is everything. \ La familia lo es todo.

I had this huge number that I sang to close the first act, and by the end of that song I had to do this big note, starting with my regular voice and then hitting falsetto.

I have a wide range as a singer, so I do that sort of thing all the time. However, toward the middle of the song, I felt my voice waning, disappearing slowly, as if somebody was turning the volume down on my voice. I'd never had that feeling before and I pray I never experience it again: I was about to sing this big note, but no matter how hard I tried, all that came out of me was air. I opened my mouth and nothing. Just silence.

Obviously, everybody freaked out. But this is the magic of Broadway: when something like this happens to one of the entertainers, people in the cast are trained to adjust even in the middle of a show. Our stage manager knew exactly what was going on and immediately turned over the cast. Certain cast members are prepared to be understudies to others, and that's exactly what happened.

I was standing onstage with no sound coming out, the lights went off, and the stage manager said, "Yeah, Jon, we got it." He switched me out of the cast and gave me the phone number for one of the best throat doctors in the city. "Go to this person right now," he urged, "and see what's going on with you."

I felt disappointed in myself, and in the fact that I couldn't finish the show. However, I knew that I had no choice but to see this doctor and hope he could help me. I was terrified. If I lost my voice, my career—everything I'd worked so hard to achieve— would be over, just like that.

When the doctor examined me, he said, "Your vocal cords are very strained. You've really worn them out, but I think you'll be okay. It's probably just vocal exhaustion. What brought this on?"

When I told the doctor about everything I was doing, he looked at me like I was insane. "Well, that's the reason you're here," he said. "You're doing far too much."

The doctor gave me a cortisone shot and these instructions: "You're going to immediately feel like you can sing like a bird, but you're going to keep your mouth shut for a whole day," he said. "I don't even want you to talk for the next twenty-four hours. You're going to take some other medicine, too. Then we'll see."

I followed his instructions to a T, I was so petrified. Fortunately, three days of rest did the trick; I was able to return and finish my run in *Grease*.

Despite this scare, performing the role of Danny Zuko on Broadway was another career highlight because it taught me so much about entertainment. I walked away from that production with the experience of having mastered the ability to inhabit a role, to truly act and feel and sing as if I were someone else instead of myself. It was also the beginning of really understanding that my body was my instrument, and that by no means could I ever treat it so carelessly again.

From that point onward, I was determined to bring my new acting skills to my live performances. All the world was a stage, and I was determined to be the best all-around entertainer I could be, no matter what form that took.

CHAPTER SIXTEEN
Love Can Make You a Better Person

Shortly after my stint on Broadway, I turned my attention to promoting my new Spanish CD, *Amor*. When EMI had proposed the album I thought it was a great idea. The reality of my career at that point was that my celebrity status and recognition factor in the Latin market was much bigger than it was in the Anglo market, so there was a lot to capitalize on by releasing an album in Spanish.

Amor was a concept album, and the songs that made up its content were the result of a deliberate strategy between my management team and the record executives. Emilio especially wanted to do an album that had the fully orchestrated flavor of something Frank Sinatra would have done, but in Spanish. His rationale for doing this was that it would give my career more depth and I would be seen as more than just a pop singer.

I was on board with this idea. In my heart, I still loved jazz singing. I thought the album we wrote and produced reflected the influence of singers like Sinatra, Tony Bennett, and Ella

Fitzgerald, yet had enough of a pop flavor for the songs to make it on the radio.

Perhaps nothing attached to touring for that album was more exciting than being invited to perform with the great Luciano Pavarotti, arguably the most famous classical tenor in history. I hadn't studied Pavarotti in school, but I had a lot of respect for classical music and training because that's how I was trained as a singer when I went to college.

As a baritone tenor, I did a lot of classical songs, including two operettas when I was in college, so I respected it and understood what talent and technique it took to sing like Pavarotti. The concert took place on a beautiful night near Pavarotti's home in Modena, Italy, in an outdoor amphitheater. We were backed by a 120-piece orchestra and sang for thousands of people.

Standing on that outdoor Italian stage next to Pavarotti as he started to sing "Granada" in Spanish, I heard that instrument coming out of the other man's huge body and was completely blown away. I had to forcibly remind myself to come back to my senses to make sure I came in at the right time during the song.

When I started singing next to him, I glanced over and saw that Pavarotti was nearly a foot away from his microphone. I was practically swallowing mine just to match the power of his voice! But it was a picture-perfect moment as our voices blended, and I still love watching the video of that performance.

I had been planning to do one of the songs off *Amor* called "Alma Con Alma," one of the best songs written in Cuban American history, at that concert. Pavarotti heard the song in rehearsal and liked it, but then he said, "You know what, Jon? You should do one of your own songs, one that really showcases what you can do."

Pavarotti told me this with such quintessentially Italian passion that he easily convinced me that I should change the song at the last minute. We got the orchestration of "Angel" just in time for me to be able to rehearse it for the show. I will never forget how Pavarotti wanted to make sure I also got a chance to shine that night.

As it turned out, *Amor* was appropriately named, for my relationship with Mari, which had started as a blind date and gradually grown into a friendship, was starting to catch fire during this time—much to the initial dismay and the resistance of her family.

By now I was in my mid-thirties and tired of my previous patterns in relationships with women. I had made a decision to examine my behavior and try to become a better partner to any woman I became seriously involved with next.

One day, I happened to walk into the office of Emilio's assistant, Frank Amadeo, and saw Mari there. It took me by surprise; our last encounter had been a blind date. "What are you doing here?" I asked.

"I just started working for Frank Amadeo," Mari said.

"Oh, that's great," I said.

I was traveling so much that it was nearly a year before I was in the office again and realized Mari was now there full-time. This time she really caught my attention.

What set Mari apart from the many other women I'd dated since my divorce? It was truly a mutual attraction of personalities as well as our physical chemistry. Mari was beautiful and sexy, no question, and she and I shared a Cuban American heritage and held many values in common, but it was her spirit that fascinated me. She never let anything bring her down—and that is still true today: Mari always finds a way to bounce back, even from the darkest moments, with a smile and a positive attitude. I saw that quality in her on day one and I've admired it ever since.

She was eleven years younger than I was, but because of her connection with the entertainment business through her work as a dancer and choreographer, and now in the office of Estefan Enterprises, she was sensitive and savvy when it came to dealing with people in the entertainment business. She wasn't easily intimidated, and she had a mind of her own.

The first time I asked Mari out to lunch, in March 1995, she said no. "I'm dating someone else," she explained.

Later, I discovered that, even though Mari was interested in me, she had refused me because she was scared. I had a reputation with women, especially in Miami, and she didn't want to get hurt. Her father, thankfully, intervened.

"Why don't you go out with him?" he said. "It's just lunch. Why don't you say yes?"

"No. Why should I?" Mari replied. "I know what he's going through and what he's like."

"So what?" her father said. "It's just lunch. Talk to him!"

I think Mari's dad pushed her to go out with me because she'd just started working for Estefan Enterprises and he didn't want her to pass up the opportunity for a friendship. He probably assumed, given the difference in our ages and stages of life, that nothing would ever develop between Mari and me.

I had asked her to lunch on March 31. The very next day, April 1, Mari called me to say, "So, look, are we going to lunch or not?"

"What do you mean?" I asked, baffled. "You told me you couldn't go."

"April Fool's," she said.

That was the beginning of a relationship that quickly snowballed. We grew closer and closer, and as we did, I knew by instinct that this relationship, this woman, was unique.

Before too long, however, Mari's family started to panic. She had never been serious about a man before. Now they were seeing changes in her—primarily an increase in independence, between her work life at Estefan Enterprises and the time she spent with me—and those changes scared them. They began to express disapproval of our relationship, not only because they thought I was too old for her, but because of my career.

I could understand this on a certain level. I was a recording artist who'd been around, and they thought I was a player.

The trouble was, the more I tried to show them how serious I was about the relationship, the more stubborn Mari's parents became about us being together. They tried to call a halt to things altogether. "We don't want you to see this guy," Mari's father told her.

I called him to ask why. "You're the one who told her to have lunch with me," I pointed out.

"I know," he said. "But, ultimately, I don't think you guys are right for each other. I don't want to see you hurt my daughter."

"I'm beginning to love your daughter," I protested. "Anyway, isn't it really up to her? She's an adult. Why are you the one trying to end things? I'm sorry, but there's nothing I can do. As long as she wants to be with me, I'm not going to stop."

"I just think it's for the best. I'm her father," he said.

I hung up, feeling frustrated and angry. At the same time, I understood. Mari's parents were trying to protect her. Ours is a culture where family ties are important, and the umbilical cord goes beyond whatever age you are.

Eventually, the issues with Mari's family got so bad that I was the one who decided to end things. The final straw was her mother being so distraught that she told Mari to break up with me or she was going to have a nervous breakdown and die. Mari was upset all the time, torn between me and her family. I couldn't see any way to resolve things and I was ready to give up.

"The last thing I want you to do is go through all this heartache," I explained, and told her I thought we should end things.

Mari understood. It was painful for both of us, but we were determined to do the best thing for her family and move on.

I was about to go to New York on a promotional run for *Amor*, and then I was going to Italy to sing with Pavarotti. In the middle of my promotional trip to New York, Mari called me.

"Look, Jon," she said. "I don't care what my parents think. I don't want to end this. I'm in love with you, and at the end of the day, this is my life. Eventually my parents will understand this is what I want."

"Are you sure?" I said. "I'm older and I can handle your parents disapproving of me. I can just walk away. But you're the one who's going to have to deal with how intensely your family will react to this decision."

"I'm absolutely sure," she said fiercely. "Let's be together. I'll tell my parents eventually. Just not right now."

This was the first time I'd seen this aggressive side of Mari. When she was passionate about making something happen, she would stop at nothing. I was overjoyed by her passion and conviction despite my worries about her having to be so secretive. I knew that would put a huge strain on her and might just ruin her relationship with her family forever.

Over the next few weeks, we saw each other on the sly. Mari had to lie to her parents all the time. It only took a few weeks for her family to catch on that our relationship was ongoing, however, because by then I was known everywhere in Miami.

They weren't happy. She again promised to break things off with me.

In Mari, I had finally found a true partner, and I was not about to let her go. I loved her more than any woman I'd ever been with. So when I decided that I was going to propose to Mari, it felt right and completely natural.

I was in Mexico for the Acapulco Music Festival. Impulsively, I went shopping and, in a jewelry store before Mari arrived, I bought her a beautiful diamond ring and had my publicist ask the chef at a popular restaurant to put the ring in a frozen dessert.

Mari and I spent the afternoon together and then went out to dinner. I was anxious and excited, since I knew there was still a chance she'd turn my proposal down because of the struggle with her family. At any point, she could bolt and tell me to forget about being together.

It was a beautiful, moonlit evening. When Mari found the ring in the dessert, I got down on one knee and said, "Mari, will you marry me?"

That's when I knew what Mari really wanted. She didn't think twice; she just said yes. Then she laughed and cried at the same time, and I nearly did the same.

She had to leave the next day. As we were kissing good-bye, she said, "Don't worry. I'll figure this out."

She still hadn't told her parents we were together, so she took the ring, but hid it somewhere in her bedroom. Meanwhile, I continued promoting *Amor* all over the world, wondering what would happen next.

In those pre-Twitter days, Mari and I managed to keep our engagement a secret from the Mexican tabloids. We even escaped the usual photographers and gossip columnists in Miami, probably because I continued to live a fairly normal, unassuming life. I never created a lot of attention, seldom traveling in a limo with an entourage, so we were able to get through several months without people noticing.

During this time, Mari and I bought a new house on the beach near the one I had bought for my parents, and she began to remodel it bit by bit. Although our friends and my parents knew about our engagement and were cautiously supportive, they were worried because Mari's family was still in the dark. They felt like we were going about things the wrong way. In retrospect, I know they were right, but sometimes love can be impulsive.

Lo and behold—and not at all surprisingly—Mari's parents

eventually put two and two together. Mari had been trying to pick the right time to tell them, but the right moment never came. Instead, one day Mari's mother spotted us leaving my house. It was an uncomfortable moment, to say the least, as Mari's mother screamed at Mari that she had to leave with her, and Mari did.

In the aftermath of her mother's fury over being deceived, Mari was shaken to the core. "I don't know how to do this," she said, crying about it with me later. "We have to just leave town and tell them we're going to elope."

"All right," I said, trying to soothe her. "Whatever you want, we'll do."

I booked a flight to London, and Mari called her parents to tell them we were leaving. "Either somewhere before or after our trip, we're going to get married. Whether you approve or not, it's going to happen. Jon and I love each other."

That was the tipping point for her parents. They finally realized that our love was real and immediately got in touch with her. "Come back," her father pleaded. "Listen, we'll work this out. We realize now how you really feel."

Her brother, too, got on the phone. "Please don't do this," he said. "There's got to be another way."

"This is between me and Mari," I told him. "This is what she wants to do. I love her, and this is the path we've chosen."

Finally, they persuaded us to return from London, unmarried. I began to get to know her family one baby step at a time. The first step was a peace-making dinner at their house, where Mari's father greeted me with a hug.

"I'm really sorry," he said immediately.

Mari's mother took longer to warm up to me. She was quiet and curt over dinner, but she had come around. She realized they were in the wrong, and that if she continued to try and change Mari's mind, she would lose her daughter.

As we talked over dinner, I saw once again how similar

Mari's family's values were to my own. Her father had just opened his first cigar shop, with Mari's brother. Her mom was a real estate agent and worked hard as well, managing various buildings. They understood what it meant to make sacrifices and work long hours to get ahead.

Her parents couldn't be better in-laws. Once they got to know me, and to see how I treated their daughter and the kind of family man I am, they started supporting us 1000 percent in everything we've done together.

I feel like that was when my real courtship of Mari started, as we got to know each other in the context of our families. That's why the album *Amor* means so much to me, because it came out while Mari and I were going through these issues, and the album is about love in all of its joyful, painful, complicated aspects.

A*mor* was released just in time to make the 1995 Grammy ballot, and sure enough, it landed a nomination for Best Latin Pop Album—and won!

I didn't take anyone to the awards ceremony that year. Still, I was happy and excited that night, and thrilled, of course, when I won my second Grammy. I had come a long way since the first Grammy Award, experiencing growing pains as an adult and reaching the crossroads where I had to decide whether or not to move forward with the relationship blossoming between Mari and me.

In addition, *Amor* was an important CD for me as an artist. Obviously, it was important in the sense that it earned a Grammy, but musically it was also a huge step forward. The album had been beautifully orchestrated by two prominent producers and arrangers, Juanito Marquez and Hector Garrido, and produced by Emilio. I was extremely proud of it, and still am. I'm grateful to Emilio for the idea of doing that album to begin with, challenging me to return to my jazz roots and the techniques I'd learned in college.

There were a lot of tremendous songs on that CD, but my favorite was *"Entre Cuatro Paredes."* For me, that song still ranks among the top five I've written throughout my career. It took me a long time to figure the song out, but once I did, I knew it captured exactly what was going on in my heart, my mind, and my spirit at the time.

In *"Entre Cuatro Paredes,"* I managed to write lyrics that expressed the culmination of life events that led to a new place in my life. I expressed my feelings in the aftermath of my divorce, as well as the spiritual connection I had with my father due to his profound love and influence in my life. This song also reflected the solitary hours I experienced while traveling, and the time I was dealing with the rigors of being on Broadway.

Mari and I were married in 1997. Over the eighteen months of our engagement, the paparazzi slowly caught on, but she was very grounded and cool with the fact that photographers were apt to pop up in unexpected places. Most of my fans took the news in a positive way as well.

We had bought our home in Miami Beach and had been slowly remodeling it, so it was ready by the time we were married. We had an all-out wedding in Coral Gables at the Church of the Little Flower and a reception in a Miami hotel. The five hundred guests included friends, family, and many people associated with my career, including Charles Koppelman and other record management executives and several Latin artists.

I didn't sing at the wedding—instead, we hired a great local band, and Emilio got onstage and played some percussion. Toward the end of the wedding, more and more musicians got onstage and it turned into a lively jam session. I couldn't have asked for a better celebration of my love for Mari and the start of our new life together.

When I reflect on my career now, I realize that my personal growth has always been entwined with my career. Maturing as a man led me to mature as an artist—and becoming a successful artist gave me the confidence to be the man I wanted to become.

Love had made me a better person. Now I was preparing for the next, more adult phase of my life, and that phase was coming fast.

PART III

Learning to Fly Solo

CHAPTER SEVENTEEN
Be a Servant to the Process

Ironically, many of our wedding guests were part of my SBK/EMI family, and that day would be the last time I'd ever see them. My carefully constructed career was about to come crashing down around my ears.

My next project for SBK/EMI was an English-language album. Mari had stopped working with Frank Amadeo and the Estefans and was helping me with the next stage of my career, as I figured out how to create and produce the new CD. I wanted to work with Miguel Morejon again. Then Don Rubin at EMI asked, "Jon, if you had a wish list of people at EMI you might want on your team this time, who would it be?"

"I'm a huge fan of Jimmy Jam and Terry Lewis," I said at once. It had always been one of my dreams to work with these talented men, who were producers for Janet Jackson and had worked with many other great artists, including Prince.

So Don reached out to them, and Jimmy Jam and Terry Lewis agreed to work with me on half of that record. It was a tremendous experience. I traveled to their home turf in Minneapolis, where we produced the record right smack in the middle of winter. SBK had once again given me a decent budget to work with, which was a good thing, since these artists were in such high demand. I had a wonderful time working with Jimmy Jam and Terry Lewis in their studio, and it was exciting to be exposed to a new way of collaborating and producing songs. To this day, I still exchange correspondence with them.

At that point in my career, Emilio and the SBK producers left the executive production of the album up to me. It was my job to ensure that the album wasn't schizophrenic, with the songs I'd written with Miguel for this album clashing with the ones I'd put together with Jimmy Jam and Terry Lewis. I succeeded in finding a connecting spirit holding the album together. The production of that CD was a fantastic process overall and I loved the final result.

I was especially thrilled with the first single, "Too Late, Too Soon," and knew it had the full support of the top executives at SBK, whom by now I'd known for five years. Their aim—and mine—was to link my success as an artist in Hispanic markets with *Amor* to my international Anglo connections.

Like clockwork, the company released the single ahead of the album and the marketing machinery kicked into gear. I had just finished promoting *Amor* throughout Latin America; now I went to Europe and Canada to promote "Too Late, Too Soon" and my next English-language album.

I'd returned to Miami briefly during that tour when Emilio called to deliver the news marking not only the demise of my career with SBK, but the end of the careers of many other artists who were part of that label as well.

"SBK has shut their doors," he said. "They're bankrupt."

I'd had no idea that was going to happen. Neither did anyone else. It all happened that suddenly, and it was shocking to us all.

As I faced that first shock of cold water to my face heralding the huge changes coming in the music industry, all I could think was, "Now what?"

The answer to that question was simple: everything stopped. No more promotional tour, no more television appearances. The record dropped off the charts. That was it. SBK had closed its doors, and all of its property was distributed or confiscated by its parent companies. That included every project in the works and everything SBK artists had produced so far—including my songs. All future royalties would go to pay off the company's debts. I would never see another penny for the songs I'd written and sung for SBK.

When I first heard the news, I was terrified. How could my career be over, just like that? I didn't want to face up to the truth that this was really happening. It was comparable to a divorce, the kind where your spouse says, "Listen, you've been loving and kind, and I've known you for a long time now, but it doesn't matter. I'm divorcing you."

You can't believe you're being abandoned, and you're left in a black hole of insecurity. I asked myself over and over again what would happen now to the career I'd established, afraid that I'd lose everything I'd worked so hard to achieve. In a flash, I began questioning all of my past choices: maybe I should have saved more money, made a different album, or stayed on my own instead of signing with Emilio. I even wondered if somehow the bad karma I deserved after my poor behavior toward Jo Pat was coming back to take revenge on me.

Meanwhile, I had to struggle to remain calm on the outside and felt increasingly isolated because I couldn't really talk to anyone about what I was feeling. I didn't want to worry my new wife, so I tried to keep a positive attitude around her. I also felt like it was essential to keep up a front with other music executives and musicians. They did the same with me. We were all too busy putting up a front with our colleagues, with everyone we talked to, making believe that everything was okay when of course everything was wrong.

One of the questions I also asked myself repeatedly during this time was whether I could have done something differently to protect myself. I know now that the answer is no. In retrospect, I understand that this event heralded the dramatic changes sweeping through the music industry in 1998 that I, like many artists, didn't see coming at the time. These changes are most clearly linked to Napster, a file-sharing application developed by a pair of teenagers that allowed people to download music from computers and MP3 music files. Instead of buying music, you could suddenly access songs at home—for free. Napster was "officially" launched in May 1999, but if it hadn't been that app, it would have been another. The Internet was radically changing the way we did everything.

At first, the heads of the major record labels tried to file a lawsuit against Napster for breach of copyright. Whatever happened legally, however, didn't change the fact that global record sales were dipping to new lows and more and more people were downloading songs for free. The world had changed and it wasn't going to change back.

I was more fortunate than many artists, in the sense that I didn't lead a lavish lifestyle. My background as a working-class musician, coupled with my instinctive survivor's mentality, helped inch me out of panic mode. If ever there was a time for me to be resilient, this was it. I was lost and had to find myself again—fast.

Probably more than anyone else, my father helped me during this time. His stance was always to listen to whatever I had to say, and then he'd usually tell me, "Jon, keep doing what you're doing. Stay focused and stay strong. You've gotten this far being the person you are and the kind of artist that you are. Don't waver." Then he'd wrap it up by reminding me that God was with me. "Believe in yourself and in the Holy Spirit."

It took me a while to shift into gear, but little by little I did it. With my father's help, and with Mari by my side, I reminded myself that I was the same person with the same passions—only wiser and more experienced now. Yes, the music business had changed, but I was still a hardworking artist with the gifts God had given me. I was determined to rebuild my career from the ground up.

I went into stealth mode as I organized my resources and thought about how to successfully relaunch my career. The first thing I did was find a business manager. I had been working with Juan Carlos Sanchez since 1994; now I decided to turn to my friend Jose Estefan, Emilio's brother, and I asked him to help manage my income. For the moment, I would be stable financially, thanks to money coming in from touring and endorsements, plus the investments my parents had made on my behalf and my own savings. In addition, I was still working at Estefan Enterprises, collaborating with various artists to produce their songs and continually writing new songs of my own.

The artists I worked with at Emilio's studio included Mandy Moore, who was very talented. She'd had a busy career as an actress but was embarking on a new venture as a singer. I did background vocals and coached her; Mandy was well protected by her family and very focused and serious.

Ironically, around this time I also worked with Lindsay Lohan. Like Mandy, Lindsay was very young, perhaps no more than seventeen, and a driven personality. However, Lindsay wasn't quite prepared to be a recording artist. We did demos for her and her voice had a lot of potential, but she didn't finish the project. Even so, I never would have predicted the wild and restless life Lindsay would lead. It is only now, looking back, that I see that the main difference between Mandy and Lindsay was the kind of guidance they had at that point in their careers. Most teen entertainers need to be surrounded by adults who will guide them carefully through life until they're mature enough to handle the attention that comes with being in the media spotlight.

Another talented entertainer who collaborated with the team at Estefan Enterprises was Marc Anthony. Like Gloria and me, he was a crossover artist in the nineties. He went on to forge an even stronger career as a Latin artist because of his deep connection to salsa and other types of tropical music.

Marc came into the studio and played a whole bunch of songs he wanted to include on his next record. As we sat together, he began singing along with the demos, belting out these songs and asking our opinion of them. His material was amazing. Beyond that, Marc's voice is a powerhouse instrument, and he uses it so effortlessly that I was completely blown away by what a great singer he is.

Two of the greatest female artists I had the opportunity to meet during that time were Jennifer Lopez and Shakira. One collaboration went smoothly. The other definitely did not.

Even before I met her, I felt like I had gotten to know Jennifer Lopez through watching her on the big screen. I admired her acting, and I was proud of what she had accomplished already as a Hispanic American woman.

In person, Jennifer is everything she appears to be as a singer, actress, and *American Idol* judge: a sweet, sexy, charming, extremely talented woman. She has that magical allure that made every guy she worked with fall a little bit in love with her. She wanted us to be attracted to her, and flirted to ensure that, but she was also extremely honest about wanting our guidance.

Tommy Mottola, the head of Sony and a good friend of Emilio's, had discovered Mariah Carey, married her, and helped make her career. Now he'd signed Jennifer Lopez. I was lucky enough to collaborate with her on "Baila," the first song that introduced her as a Sony pop artist.

While I was working with Jennifer as a producer and songwriter, she turned to me with the most beautiful smile at one point and said, "Look, I need your help. I know I have a long way to go as a singer, but I'm here, and I want to be the best pop artist I can be."

I'll never forget that moment, because Jennifer was so honest and determined to work hard. Her candor and transparency inspired me to root even harder for her success, which she has achieved beyond all measure.

With Mandy and Jennifer, as with most singers I've coached and produced throughout my career, I did everything I could to make them feel I was in their corner. Rather than walking in as an artist, I chose to be accommodating, to call upon everything I had learned as an educator, songwriter, and producer to become a servant to the process of making music. I wanted to coach them to stretch their own capabilities comfortably, constantly pushing them to reach deeper and pull out better notes without feeling intimidated during recording sessions.

To this day, I love sitting in the production booth, recording as many takes as possible, while always boosting the confidence of the artist, saying, "Great, that's really great. Let's just do one more take now."

During production, I have a cheerleader's personality, even jumping up and down to pump that person up if I have to; I become a motivator and an educator again, helping singers break down the sounds and make them even richer. After every take, I'll ask the singer, "Okay, how did you feel about that take? Did you like it?"

Even if the singer says yes, and has a look of confidence, I'll say, "That's great. Let's do another take."

If the singer seems frustrated, I'll suggest things for them to try on the next take, always saying, "That sounded great. Let's try this now. Pretend you're punching yourself in the stomach and dropping your jaw, or raise your hands when you hit that last note." I'll do whatever is necessary to encourage singers to sing with their entire bodies and confidently take vocal risks.

Jennifer and Shakira may appear similar beneath the glare of the media spotlight—both sexy, talented Latina singers—but whereas Jennifer comes across as warm and welcoming in most situations, Shakira is assertive and all business. While things didn't go smoothly between us at first, I learned a great deal from her.

My first working experience with Shakira wasn't vocal coaching or production, but collaborating on a songwriting project. Shakira brought a song to the studio that needed to be completed. I started working on it, just fixing the song up here and there, adding a new section and, because I always finish what I start, making a demo of the final product to be sure Shakira was okay with it.

I was communicating with Shakira through her musical director because Shakira was doing a lot of touring at the time, and I was trying to keep her informed as to what I was doing with this song. I never got a response. I wasn't particularly bothered by that; people sometimes don't respond if they're busy.

Eventually, Shakira got in touch with me. The song still didn't have lyrics; she showed me some of the lyrics she'd written in Spanish, and meanwhile I was working on the song in English.

Finally, when I went to her apartment to hear what she had, she showed me her Spanish version. "Shakira, did you listen to that demo I sent?" I asked, and from whatever she said, I concluded that she had, and that she was okay with it.

I left that meeting to complete the song. About eight months later, I got a call from Emilio's publisher. "Jon, I have good news and bad news," she said.

The good news was that Alejandro Fernández had heard the demo I did for Shakira and wanted to use it on one of his albums.

"The bad news is that Shakira says she never had any idea you completed the song, and doesn't want to give you credit."

Of course I didn't have any written agreement with Shakira. The only option was for me to call her myself to decide how she and I would split the songwriting credit and, by extension, the royalties. Shakira wasn't interested in splitting anything, it turned out. "Jon, I'm sorry," she said, "but I never agreed to give you credit or approved of that."

I sputtered, completely taken aback by her refusal. "Look, I understand that most of that song was yours," I said, "and maybe there was a misunderstanding, but all I want is a certain percentage of royalties for the song. Okay? Are we straight on that?"

"No," she said. "I want the whole song."

Up to that day, I had never gotten as upset with anybody professionally as I did with Shakira. By the end of the conversation I was screaming at her over the phone. "What the hell are you talking about?" I yelled. "Are you kidding me? Or are you crazy? I understand most of the song is yours, but this guy heard this demo with the portion I wrote, and that's what he wants!"

Shakira finally said, "Okay, Jon. Don't scream, don't get like that. Lower your voice."

"I can't lower my voice when you're telling me something that doesn't make sense to me!" I shouted.

I have to hand it to her: Shakira stayed cool the whole time. In the end, she said, "Jon, look, I'll give you ten percent of the royalties, but it's important to me that my name appears as the sole writer on that song."

I realized then that, to Shakira, there was a professional business principle attached to her hard-line position, so I agreed. "I'm okay with that," I said. "I don't need my name on the song as long as you give me ten percent." Then we hung up, my hand still shaking.

Since then, Shakira and I have made our peace and worked

together many times. What I took from that encounter was a respect for Shakira's relentless commitment to actually fight for what was important to her, which at that point was how she wanted to represent herself as a writer. Shakira is a tough businesswoman, which is part of the reason she's had such a successful career.

From that moment on, I was much more careful about how I wrote songs with other people. Shakira knew how to fight for herself, and that would become increasingly important to me in the future.

Ricky Martin was around the studios during that time as well. I had first met Ricky in New York when I was performing in *Grease*. He had been brought to New York to headline a Broadway production of *Les Misérables*.

I had immediately appreciated Ricky's calm, soothing spirit during our first meeting. Besides being a great entertainer, he has an extremely welcoming personality and always speaks with a lot of depth. He's in tune with the people around him and, more importantly, with his own spirituality. Perhaps that's why things went the way they did when he wanted one of my songs—the song that would become the megahit "She's All I Ever Had" and, in its Spanish version, "Bella."

Ricky had begun his career at age twelve with the Spanish group Menudo, followed by his Spanish-language solo albums. In 1998, he was working on his first English CD, a crossover project for Sony, and there was a huge buzz about him in the music industry. By that time, Ricky and I had met many times at industry events. Ricky was working with Robi Rosa, who I often saw around the studio; he had recently released "La Vida Loca" and it was already making a huge splash on the radio.

All in all, it was great being in the studio again. Emilio's production company was busier than it had ever been, with up to fifty writers, producers, and arrangers working on the premises at any one time. I loved collaborating with so much great talent every day. At the same time, it was an unnerving transitional period. Every day at the studio, I'd ask myself, "What am I doing here? What is the purpose of this journey?"

Meanwhile, Emilio approached Sony Music on my behalf, where he was able to broker a contract for me. I immediately started writing songs that would become part of my first Sony project, "Better Part of Me," which would be released in 2000. As pleased as I was that Emilio had pulled this off on my behalf, my mentality had changed. I understood now that the music business was uncertain. I didn't want to lose confidence in myself or lose my faith in the people I worked with, but I had seen firsthand how situations could crumble so easily. Even while I was walking into the deal with Sony and bringing all of this outward swagger with me, I was walking on eggshells from that point forward and always looking for sturdier ground.

As was my customary habit, I'd go to the studio every day to bounce certain songs off whoever happened to be around. One morning, I met up with my friend, the writer and producer George Noriega. He was really excited because he'd just finished going through some musical ideas with Robi Rosa for Ricky's album.

George started playing some of those ideas for me—just fragments of melodies at that point. Not many lyrics or anything, just what I like to call "really cool mumblings." Each one was just a few seconds long. One of those mumblings really jumped out at me. George said, "Yeah, I like that, too."

"Let's finish that song," I suggested. As always, I liked to complete demos of any song I was working on, to sort of seal them in place.

What I liked about this particular fragment was the combination of the riff George was playing and the melodic ideas of Robi Rosa. Robi was terrifically talented; if he felt a connection with a

writer, he could literally start humming something within seconds. That was the case with these ideas.

George and I made appointments to finish the song together.
Eventually, I completed the lyrics, just kind of picking out words
from the mumblings Robi had taped, and George finished the
music. That song became "She's All I Ever Had." I did a demo of
it so I could hear it back, singing it as if the song were written for
me. I liked it so much that I started playing it for other people
around the studio, beefing up the demo a little more.

Robi hadn't yet heard the song, but he knew George and I
had completed it, so he asked George to play him the demo the
next time he was at the studio. His reaction was, "Wow, man."

"Yeah," George said enthusiastically, "Look how great Jon
sounds on this song."

At that exact moment, as George reported it to me later, Robi
got a call from Angelo Medina, who was his manager as well as
Ricky's, and Robi said, "Hey, wow, I just finished hearing this
song that Jon Secada wrote using one of my ideas. George and
Jon completed it, and the song sounds amazing."

Robi got really quiet on the phone as he listened to whatever
Angelo was telling him, then said, "But, Angelo, it's not like that,
man. No, no, no. Yeah, I know I'm here to write for Ricky. I know
that, but it's not like that, man. It's not like that."

Apparently, Angelo had realized that, if Robi thought the
song was that good, it probably was—and Ricky should sing it.
Angelo asked Robi to send the song to him and Ricky. Sure
enough, Ricky fell in love with my song.

I didn't know any of this at the time, of course. I was out touring. When I came back to Miami, Emilio approached me and
said, "Look, Jon, we have a little situation here. At the end of the
day, you control it."

He told me that Ricky wanted "She's All I Ever Had" for his
new English-language album, and that it was my call whether I

wanted to give Ricky permission or not. Emilio understood that I really wanted to put the song on my own record—that's why I'd completed it and done a demo—and of course Ricky and everyone else associated with Sony knew that as well. We were label mates at this point.

Emilio didn't tell me what to do, but he used his influence in that subtle-Emilio-way. He called me into his office and said, "You don't have to do anything, Jon. You can use the song, you can put it on your record, and this song could be a huge success for you or not. But Ricky really, really loves the song. Everybody in his camp really loves the song, too."

He also reminded me that "La Vida Loca" was already a huge hit on the radio, then added, "Talking to you as an artist, I would say, hey, you should use the song yourself. But as your publisher, I would say you should give this song to Ricky. He loves it enough for it to be a single, and it would be a second single after 'La Vida Loca.' I can tell you right now that Sony will be putting a lot of marketing and promotional juice behind Ricky's project, so it'll go far with him. It could be a number one hit for you, but it will definitely be a number one hit for Ricky, with the kind of push he's getting from the record company."

Honestly, that was all I needed to hear. In the end, I wanted what was best for the song, I really did. So I told myself that I'd come up with other stuff that was just as good, and gave up "She's All I Ever Had" to Ricky.

I ended up being part of the production team for the song, too. It was a little outside of Ricky's vocal comfort zone, so I acted as coproducer and helped him with background vocals. He did a great job on "She's All I Ever Had," and it topped the charts in 1999. In 2001, I earned a BMI award for Best Pop Songwriter for writing "She's All I Ever Had," and the same award for the Spanish version "Bella" in the BMI Latin category.

To this day, whenever I hear "She's All I Ever Had" on the

radio, I crank it up, I'm so happy and proud of it. I was proud of what I had achieved as a songwriter, and of the fact that I was doing what I loved to do. How many people got to say that about their lives?

At the same time, I was acutely aware that I wasn't satisfied just writing songs. Part of me was very patiently biding my time, completing songs that I hoped would make it onto my next album so that I could resume my career as an entertainer. Every day I'd take a deep breath and tell myself that I was still an established recording artist even if it felt like I was right back where I'd started. As my father often counseled me to do, I reminded myself to look at every day with new eyes as I continued believing in myself, remembering where I'd come from, and honoring how much I had achieved already.

Not long after that, we visited Tommy Mottola in New York and went to dinner at an Italian place with him. By this time, I had met Tommy many times, bumping into him the first time while he was still working at EMI. No matter how brief our meetings, it was always clear that Tommy was a driven music executive who was always focused on making the necessary decisions to boost a singer's career, even if those decisions were difficult ones. He had a long roster of artists.

At the table, Emilio and I were joined by Tommy and a couple of other top Sony executives who were going back and forth, talking to Emilio about Ricky's success with "La Vida Loca" and how he was exploding onto the scene like nobody else.

In a lot of ways it was a classic dinner scene of that time, with record executives talking about songs and artists, radio stations and marketing strategies. Emilio was a great producer for Tommy and had brought all kinds of Sony artists along in their careers, Anglo and Hispanic and whatnot, so they were enthusiastic to be there together and talking business.

At one point, Emilio mentioned the album I'd just finished.

Tommy assured me that they had a plan for me, but then the conversation quickly moved on.

I have to admit it: I felt a little terrible. I wasn't the "it" artist of the moment. It was Ricky Martin's turn now. Emilio had invited me because I was a good wingman. Besides being a recording artist, I'd been involved in writing and producing a lot of songs they were talking about at that table.

As I listened to the conversations, I could hear the drumbeat of change coming. The shape of the music industry was rapidly shifting beneath our feet. I was suddenly glad to be there. By embracing the opportunities to work with so many gifted artists as a vocal coach, songwriter, and producer, I was allowing myself to become a servant to the process of making great music. I became a student of Emilio's, too, especially when I watched how he handled meetings with executives and learned how he presented and sold his ideas to the highest music executives in the land. It was a great workshop and I took joy in the process. Even better, I understood now that I was absorbing knowledge I would use later, when it was time for me to diversify my career and recreate myself again and again.

CHAPTER EIGHTEEN
Fatherhood Is the Best Part of Me

Marriage was less of a shock to me than it was to Mari, because I'd lived with a woman before and she'd led a sheltered life. Even after eighteen months of dating, though, we still had surprises in store when we moved in together.

The main issue we had to contend with was our opposite personalities. Yes, opposites attract—unless they try to live together. Then it's one battle after another. Mari and I had come from similar backgrounds, but where she was openly emotional and quick to express her opinions, I tended to come across as laid-back and even, at times, passive, in my attempts to avoid confrontation. Once we started living together, Mari drove me nuts with her type A, aggressive personality at times—it was too much like what I'd seen in my own parents—and I made her nearly insane with what she saw as my reluctance to assert, or even express, my desires.

I was doing everything in my power to avoid having the kind of marriage I'd seen my own parents have early on, with my father going off at the least provocation and my mother squaring off and giving it right back to him. Initially, I made it my goal to have the patience and communication to hold back in an argument. The problem was that Mari, in an effort to get me to communicate with her about whatever I was thinking and feeling, would push and prod me in her spirited way until I reached the boiling point and blew up.

The early years of our marriage were a huge discovery process as we struggled with our differences but made the commitment to overcome them over and over again out of our deep love for each other. I continued to hold my feelings in, or try to, and to Mari's credit she would go out of her way to get me to say whatever was inside of me, no matter what kind of protective shield I put up because the power of my own emotions could scare me.

Even though Mari and I were still learning how to live together, we had decided to have children sooner rather than later because I was already in my thirties. I remember the trip when Mari conceived our daughter. We had gone to New York City, to a party held by friends in the city, and went back to our hotel after a little too much to drink. Shortly afterward, she announced that she was pregnant.

Despite my joy, as usual, my first instinctive impulse was to fall quiet and reflect on the enormity of the moment. So many thoughts and feelings were washing over me at once. We smiled at each other and just sat quietly for a few moments, then embraced and started talking excitedly about everything that might happen from that point forward.

Fatherhood was almost like a born-again experience for me. Immediately, I wanted to change my life, to stay home rather than travel the way I had been, touring so constantly, so that I could be the kind of father I wanted to be.

Our beautiful daughter, Mikaela, was born on February 15, 1999. I was there for my daughter's birth, and I slept with Mari in her room the whole time she was in the hospital. Now I was officially the head of a family.

I could see how my parents had raised me, and I had a new respect for the hardships they'd suffered, their struggles to survive, and their perseverance as a couple. Every person, every couple, carries a world within, so it's difficult to know what's inside that world. A lot of it was revealed to me on the day my daughter was born. I think Mari and I truly became defined as people when we became parents. We were still challenging each other every day as we kept trying to express how we felt without taking things so personally, then moving on from our disagreements big and small.

After having children, Mari and I vowed to be even more intelligent as communicators. We wanted to choose our words and thoughts carefully, to be always fully conscious of what we were saying in front of our children, or to them, so that we could parent them in a way that would allow them to become whoever they wanted to become while upholding the family values of love, commitment, hard work, and compassion that we held dear. It wasn't always easy.

Once Mikaela was home, I was thrilled to help Mari any way I could, from feeding the baby to changing diapers. Luckily I was in a good position to do so during that time, since we were still wrapping up my new album for Sony and hadn't yet organized a promotional tour.

When the time came to do the video for the first single from the album in Spain, I literally did not want to leave my family. Deep down inside, I knew that after so many years of focusing on my career, I longed to focus on something else now: my personal life. The balance of my priorities had definitely shifted.

During my transition to fatherhood, Emilio had brokered a three-album deal for me with Sony. The first of those albums, *Better Part of Me*, was released in 2000.

The songs on that album were written by a variety of

collaborators. I had let myself be led in various directions while creating the songs for that CD because I was a new artist at Sony and trying once again to be a team player. In retrospect, it was probably one of the bigger mistakes of my career. Agreeing to work with so many different people in the Sony stable was a political decision, but a heartfelt one. I knew what was going on in the music industry, where things were becoming less and less favorable for artists across the board, in terms of how projects were being handled and prioritized. I have always been a bit of a chameleon, and since I was a brand-new artist with Sony, I consciously let their management team direct who I should work with, from cowriters to producers.

The result was a collage. Some songs were given to me by Tommy Mottola and involved working with Tony Moran and Ric Wake, among others. I also had a young producer, Steve Morales, with a really urban rhythm-and-blues background on some of the other songs. In all, four production teams were involved with the album.

It was the first time my friend Miguel hadn't been involved in one of my projects. He understood the pressure I was under, and he knew that I was trying to do the right thing for my career, but there was a side of him that was hurt by my decision.

I still question a lot of the choices I made on that album. The upside was that making this album gave me a chance to explore new working relationships with people I'd never met before, and there was an exciting synergy in pulling all of that together. Each of those artists brought something new to the way I made music. But as I reflect back on the process, I realize I shouldn't have given myself over so completely to the team at Sony. The minute I did that, I gave up control. The album lacked my personal stamp on it. I should have had more of an ego.

As it turned out, Sony was a much, much bigger company than EMI, and the album didn't hold up to the expectations that the company and I had for it. As opposed to being a priority with Sony as I had been with EMI, I was just another artist for Sony, plus this was the beginning of budget cuts across the board for most record companies. If a project didn't show promise from the first single, or if the initial marketing push was less than hugely successful, the priority level given to the project was immediately lowered.

That's what happened to *Better Part of Me*. The album didn't sink like a stone, exactly, but it wasn't a blockbuster hit, either. Things had continued to radically change in the music industry, so record executives were quick to cut their losses instead of nurturing and developing new talent, which was admittedly expensive and, by 2000, a potentially losing proposition. They were more apt to withdraw whatever marketing money had been keeping a record alive than pull out all the promotional stops to ensure its success.

Failing with *Better Part of Me* wasn't just a disappointment for me, it was one of the most frustrating moments in my career. I was completely taken aback by the record label's sudden disinterest in me, and I was angry at myself for not being able to change that. I kept hammering myself with the same tiresome questions: What could I have done differently to make this album a success? What could my management company have done better to support me?

Eventually, I decided there wasn't any point in berating myself for the choices I'd made. I had to see this as a serious wake-up call. This was the beginning of another new day for me. If I wanted to keep doing what I loved to do, I was going to have to think more independently and make different career choices. I was still signed with Sony for two more albums, but things were changing right in front of our eyes. Unless I started changing, too, my career was doomed.

From that point on, I was determined to ask more questions

and take a more hands-on approach to the day-to-day decisions about everything from producing my albums to marketing them. I was going to have to find out what the company's plans were for me and take the role of an independent hustler, someone who took charge of his own destiny, whether I was with a record label or not after this contract with Sony was up. And I was going to do all of that in light of my new role as a husband and father who wanted to travel less and live a more balanced life.

My next Sony project sprang from Tommy Mottola's idea that I should do a Christmas album. I loved the idea. Holiday-themed albums are an "evergreen" in the music industry, since the annual holiday season means there's always an easy way to market your CD.

We did the album in the classiest way possible, and it still remains one of my favorite recordings. I had worked with a great Dominican-born arranger and producer, José Antonio Molina, when he conducted the show I'd performed with Pavarotti. Now José Antonio was working with Emilio quite a bit. He was an accomplished pianist and composer, and we were fortunate to have his help when Emilio and I were choosing a collection of classic holiday songs for the album.

We knew we wanted to make a fully orchestrated record. We were also aware of the cost this kind of quality sound would entail. José Antonio said, "Listen, just give me a month, and I'll have something for you."

Having an idea of what the arrangements would be like could save us a lot of time and money. So we picked the songs, gave them to José Antonio, and went to his house a month later to hear how he'd put the songs together. There, we discovered that he'd set up a beautiful keyboard with this tremendous synthesizer and great string patch attached to it. José Antonio started playing an exact arrangement of what every song was going to sound like with a real orchestra playing.

I was flabbergasted. I'd never seen any musician do that. "Man, I don't know what to say," I managed finally. "That sounds terrific."

We had decided to do the album in the old-school recording style, with me singing with the orchestra in an isolation booth. "You're one of the few singers who could pull this off," José Antonio said.

We recorded the entire album in four days. José Antonio had written out all of the parts, and it was like I was in front of Mozart or something, just seeing José Antonio go through those arrangements with the orchestra.

Appropriately enough, we called our holiday album *The Gift*. It really was that, too, because creating *The Gift* allowed me to make a new recording while staying home with my wife and young daughter. And even after I left Sony, this album remained a staple in their catalog. It keeps on giving even today. More importantly, it's an album I'm especially proud of because I made it my way.

B ecoming a parent definitely opened a new chapter in my life. It was a huge turning point and led to a series of epiphanies about my life in music. I'd always written songs from a very soulful place and I'd always been a reflective person. Now, being a father took me even deeper into examining my life—and the lives of the people around me—from a more mature perspective.

In terms of my career, everything had come full circle. I had found the best part of myself in fatherhood. After the success of my first two albums, I had been addicted to celebrity, thinking that all I needed was one more song to hit the charts and I'd be happy. Now I realized that what my father had always told me really was true: happiness is never permanent. It is fleeting. Enjoy it while you can, and find it where you can.

I knew that it was possible to create hit songs because I had succeeded at doing that. I had enjoyed a taste of that fast life in the media spotlight. I wouldn't mind doing that again, but at the same time, my priorities were definitely different now. I was back to enjoying the process of making music in my own way, at my own pace, as I recreated myself as an entertainer who could balance a successful career with a family life.

CHAPTER NINETEEN
As the World Changes, So Must You

On September 11, 2001, I had traveled to Los Angeles as a presenter for the first all-Latin Grammy Awards. I've always been an early riser, and I'll never forget waking up to the news that the twin towers had been struck down. Like everyone, my reaction was one of disbelief, fear, and confusion.

My first concern during those crazy days after the terrorist attack was to make it home to my family in Florida. This was no easy feat, since nobody was flying anywhere. A few of my friends managed to rent cars or campers to drive back, but just as they were hitting the road, the airports opened again. As scared as I was to fly during that uncertain time, I got on the first red-eye flight leaving Los Angeles.

As soon as I was back in Miami, Emilio approached me about producing a song to collect money for the victims of 9/11. The project was an enormous undertaking and involved recording the voices of sixty Latin artists, including Christina Aguilera, José Feliciano, Jennifer Lopez, and Ricky Martin.

The song we produced was written by Emilio and the Peruvian singer-songwriter Gian Marco. Titled "The Last Goodbye," or *"El Ultimo Adios,"* it was challenging not only to sing but to produce, because we had to coordinate so many different voices on it. I was in charge of vocal production for the song, and took on that project with all of the love in my heart, once again assuming the role of coach and cheerleader for artists I admired to create a unified sound out of many voices.

Shortly after that song wrapped up, I had the opportunity to return to Broadway. For this, I have to credit my longtime agent, Jorge Pinos of William Morris. Jorge had believed in me from day one, and he'd been responsible for most of my bookings.

Jorge knew how much I'd enjoyed doing *Grease.* Now, he said, there was a new production of *Cabaret* in New York, and they were looking for someone to play the role of the emcee—the same role Joel Grey had made so popular in the movie version.

I was thrilled by the idea. This production of *Cabaret* was being directed by the great Sam Mendes, who had done a lot of films, and was choreographed by Rob Marshall, who later did the movie *Chicago.* The first time the show had played on Broadway, Alan Cumming earned a Tony Award for his role as the emcee; the person I saw in the part was Neil Patrick Harris, who played Doogie Howser on television and was one of the stars of the hit sitcom *How I Met Your Mother.*

I had no idea what to expect from *Cabaret* until the night I went to see it. I knew the music and the story, but the movie had been made in the seventies and this was a brand-new, revamped production. It was a very sexy show set in a 1930s burlesque house. In many ways, it was much racier than they could have gotten away with doing in the movies. Sam and Rob had taken the characters, the story line, and the music, stripping them all down to as raw a place as they could go.

As soon as I saw the show, I wanted to do it. I was certain that

playing the emcee role would change my life forever as an entertainer. I'd be challenged to do things I'd never done before, to get
into the mind and body of a character completely unlike me.

With *Grease*, I'd been given two weeks to prepare for the part,
then another couple of weeks to learn the choreography and every other aspect of the production. Knowing that my role in
Cabaret would be more difficult than playing Danny Zuko, I decided to travel to New York City early for coaching. The emcee
role was one of a transsexual, bisexual drug addict with a German accent, one who wore makeup, dresses, garters, and heels. I
had painted nipples and a swastika on my ass, and I'd have to
appear naked at the end of Act I. For this, I definitely needed
help.

To start with, I was determined to be in the best shape of my
life. I had stayed thin and worked out a bit since college, but had
done nothing consistent. Now I wanted to tone my body, build
muscle, and limber up for this physically demanding role. I think
this sudden shift in my thinking was part of the mental shift I
was making in seeing myself as an all-around entertainer now,
not just a singer. I wanted to do something to rattle my cage because instinctively I knew it was part of my growth process as an
independent artist to look as good as I could.

Slowly but surely, I began incorporating my workout routine
into my lifestyle as a constant reality, starting with a trainer to
find routines that worked for me. The more I got into it, the more
I realized that even if I was traveling for a gig, I had to stay on top
of my eating habits and workouts to be on top of my game. For
the past eight years, I've had a steady six-day-a-week training
regimen of running or walking, combined with weight training
and workouts for cardio and abs.

Before the official rehearsals began for *Cabaret*, I also found
an experienced acting coach, one whose specialty was working
with celebrities who were taking on Broadway roles. The coach

went beyond helping me learn my lines, pushing me to grasp the flirtatious, flamboyant persona of the character I had to play. I also worked with a diction coach. As a Latino, I found it especially tricky to master the part of speaking English with a German accent!

I'd be doing eight shows a week, and I was determined to stay healthy this time. As I'd learned from my experience in *Grease*, doing so would require discipline and luck. None of the people who'd taken on the emcee role in the past had lasted for the whole run without missing a performance or two, because the part was both vocally and physically demanding. I was expected to be moving all over the stage from the beginning to the end of the show. I made a point of eating the healthiest diet possible and rarely went out at night, determined to rest my body and my voice. I'm proud to say that I never, in seven and a half months, missed a single performance.

It was an exhilarating experience to play such a dramatically different character, a role that pushed me far outside my comfort zone as an entertainer. Still, it was a tough experience as well. Mari and I had been blessed by a second child, our son, Jon Henri, about a year before I started the show; at one point she brought the children and a nanny to the two-bedroom apartment I was staying in for a few weeks, but the show was too demanding for any of us to enjoy it much. She took the kids back to Miami and I was left on my own. It was a very solitary, lonely time. I felt like I was in a cocoon anytime I wasn't onstage, because I would just stay in the apartment on the days I had to perform. We had one day off a week, and if I didn't fly down to Miami to see my family, I walked the streets of New York City like a zombie without talking to a soul, then came back to crash. I was that tired.

In the end, though, it was worth it. Anyone who came to see me in *Cabaret* would walk away knowing I was doing something uniquely challenging, whether that person liked the show or not.

Best of all, I earned rave reviews from theater critics, even in the *New York Times*, which was icing on the cake.

More importantly, doing *Cabaret* taught me how to be much more dynamic as a vocalist, actor, and dancer all in one. I had never before thought of myself as an entertainer at that level, one who could be so multidimensional, but from that point onward in my career I made sure to incorporate that kind of depth of performance into all of my concerts and handled myself completely differently onstage.

Playing the emcee in *Cabaret* also taught me techniques for forming a more intimate connection with an audience—a close, personal bond I'd never managed to achieve before. I discovered how to really let go and put everything out there onstage. I'll always be grateful for having had that opportunity to discover and master new abilities and techniques as an all-around entertainer.

By 2003, I'd finished performing in *Cabaret* and had already started preproduction for my next album, *Amanecer*. I felt fulfilled as an entertainer and newly confident about my stage presence. My life in Miami had started to settle into a new rhythm as an entertainer, husband, and father. I knew now that I wanted to organize my world—including my drive and ambition—in a way that would satisfy not only my work ethic, but also the passion I felt for my family.

Amanecer would be the last album in the three-record deal Emilio had brokered for me with Sony. Little did I know that it would be the last album I'd ever do with a major record label—or that this album would be the final one produced with Emilio's production staff and team.

This time around, Emilio and I had decided we should do a recording in Spanish. It would be released under Sony's Crescent Moon label, Emilio's own label within Sony music. For the first time in my career, I wasn't involved in writing any of the songs.

I've always been pretty objective about the quality of my writing, and I felt the songs the other writers on the production team were offering sounded better than my own. This would be my second all-Spanish CD, after *Amor*, so I wanted to make sure I had the best Spanish-language songs possible.

Some of the songs on *Amanecer* were by Archie Peña. The Peruvian writer Gian Marco also gave me some great songs. Archie did a tremendous job of giving the record a very earthy, organic, acoustic percussion sound.

When I look back at the arrangements and the actual production breakdown on that album, I'm still awed by Archie's work. We didn't use any drums on that record at all, yet you don't miss them because of the layers of percussion he used. One of the songs, *"Si No Fuera Por Ti"* by Gian Marco, rose to become a Top 10 Latin hit.

Amanecer is a tropical album; it fused a lot of different rhythms and had none of the ballads I was used to singing. Maybe because it was such a different sound for me, I had trouble getting into singing some of the songs. One day, I'd just come back from lunch and I was having a really tough time with a particular song. Archie could see I was getting frustrated.

"What's going on?" he asked.

"I just want to make sure that I'm as dead on with this as I can be, but I'm having a problem with this song," I said.

"Come on, Jon," Archie said. "Don't give up. You're going to get it, man. You want a drink or something?"

I seldom drank when I was working, but that day I said yes. So Archie sent his assistant out for a little bottle of Scotch, and I took a sip in the booth just before I started to sing. We started to joke around, and whatever tension was in me left, just vanished completely. I sailed through that up-tempo song without a hitch.

So that became the thing for *Amanecer*: as we were laying

down the tracks, for each up-tempo song I drank a little bottle of Johnnie Walker. I printed the name of each song on the bottle I'd consumed while singing it. Maybe that's why this album is infused with a real sense of tropical fun.

I traveled for several months to promote *Amanecer*. In many ways, this promotional tour reminded me of how it had felt to promote my first album, in the sense that Emilio and I had been given a budget from Sony that covered a comprehensive radio campaign. Emilio hired a really good independent radio promoter to plug the song in Spanish to every single market in the country that hosted popular Latin radio stations, and I had fun playing at different venues and helping with the promotional campaign. I wasn't at all nervous, the way I had been with my very first album. At this point, I was experienced in the process and knew I could handle it. It was made even sweeter by the fact that I understood how quickly—and how drastically—the music industry was changing, and knew that these sorts of promotional opportunities with big record companies were drying up fast for all artists.

Afterward I came back to my family in Miami and settled into helping Emilio do production work for Crescent Moon, working as a coproducer and songwriter as we revived Miami Sound Machine using a group of teenagers. I loved being able to keep a regular schedule at the studio, because it allowed me to continue spending time at home with my children while still writing and producing.

Most importantly, I felt like my education in music was continuing. Besides listening to popular music on the radio, I met a lot of young talent at Emilio's production company. I loved collaborating with them, fusing different musical elements and styles and producing songs that could stand the test of time. It was exciting just to be in the studio and jumping in with both feet on a project, allowing myself to be completely objective in the creative process with artists whose styles were often vastly different from my own.

After a year spent in Emilio's studio—a year in which I'd focused on other artists and let my own career as an entertainer slide into the background—I knew I'd reached another fork in the road. It was time to start another new day in my career as an independent artist.

I could see the relentless progress—or changes, anyway—in the music industry, and knew my time was up with Emilio's studio. The reality was that record sales were plummeting on a monthly basis for most artists. It was 2004 and music lovers now had ready access to songs online at little or no cost. Meanwhile, executives at the big labels were being fired left and right, and artists who signed on with them couldn't be certain of the support they'd get.

Emilio and I were good friends. We still are. He and I have never had a serious argument, and Emilio and Gloria are godparents to my son. I still work with Jose Estefan, Emilio's brother, who serves as my business manager, and his wife's accounting firm does my books. I even work in Emilio's studio every so often, since it's right down the street from my house. Yet Emilio and I never had conversations about our decision to go our separate ways or any sort of official good-bye.

We were operating by instinct, as he and I had so often done. I think Emilio and I both knew that after eighteen years of working together, we had done as much as we could as a team. In light of the changes in the music world, plus where I was in my career, there was little Emilio could do to help manage my career that I didn't have the skills and experience to do on my own. It was time to consider the next phase of my career. Once again, I had to ask myself, "Now what?"

Emilio and I parted ways, but what I took away from those

eighteen years with him and still carry with me today were his incredible work ethic and his unerring instincts to really envision a future and really believe in it enough to sell it to people. That confidence comes from a willingness to change as the world is changing. I had all the tools I needed now to be truly independent.

CHAPTER TWENTY
You Can Only Fly If You Spread Your Wings

One of the first exciting opportunities to come my way as I finished working with Emilio was another theatrical show. This time, I was offered the leading role in a touring production of *Joseph and the Amazing Technicolor Dreamcoat.*

I jumped at the chance, not only because I was ready to do something different, but also because I loved the idea of throwing myself into another theatrical production. This show also represented another crossroads, in that it ended up being the last bit of work that I did with Jorge Pinos, who left William Morris soon after that.

Joseph and the Amazing Technicolor Dreamcoat had a four-month run. Although I had been cast as the lead, I handled the role easily, as this was probably the least complex show ever written by the team of Andrew Lloyd Webber and Tim Rice. The production proved to be very lighthearted but popular in touring circles, so I really had fun doing it.

At the same time, 2004 was a reflective time for me as I

pondered how to manage my career as a solo artist without any management or recording contract. I was fortunate to have Mari by my side; since leaving her job with Estefan Enterprises when we got married, she had taken on the role of being my personal executive assistant, along with managing the household and being a full-time mother to our two children.

Mari knew the inner workings of the music business really well. The question was which direction to choose for my future career path, and how we could outsource enough work so that our relationship wouldn't be overwhelmed. Instinctively, I went back to the hustle, counting on my survival skills to allow me not only to continue my life as a musician, but also to provide for my family.

It was about then that I was approached by a boutique record company that distributed jazz products. One of the founders was Dave Koz, a sax player I knew and respected. Through my publicist, Michael Caprio, I heard that Koz's company, Rendezvous Entertainment, was putting together a record of lullabies by noted artists. Dave asked if I wanted to participate by writing a song for my children.

When I agreed to the project, that was my first introduction to life as an independent artist. I wrote "Find Me in Your Dreams" for my children, and in doing so I experienced what it was like to work with a small production outlet that could cater to my needs as an established recording artist.

The experience went smoothly and gave me the impetus I needed to begin my first independent project. My plan was to return to the original blueprint of my life as a working songwriter and musician. This time I was determined to do a specialty concept record on my own, a jazz album. That's where my true passion still resided.

As a student at the University of Miami, I had developed and nurtured a love of jazz because the training taught me to think of myself as an instrumentalist—one whose instrument is his voice. My goal has always been to be the best musician possible—not just a singer, but a true musician who understands everything from reading music to theory to improvisation. Musicians have a common language and I wanted to speak it.

I had successfully achieved that goal during my metamorphosis in my college jazz studies. Now I had become the kind of entertainer who could also write songs, coach other vocalists, sing background, and produce albums, and I wanted to honor my jazz roots with an album that showcased the depth of my knowledge and the breadth of my musicianship.

I recorded the album, *Expressions*, in an old-school style, singing in a booth and using a rhythm section. The result was an organic, earthy, mostly acoustic album with heavy jazz influences, along the lines of what Norah Jones was doing at that time. It's clear when I listen to it that the album is the product of the artists I studied in college who influenced me along the way, but I also knew how successful the Norah Jones project had been—and was acutely aware that it been produced by a small record company, not a big label. Norah's success underscored what was happening in the music industry, where a lot of small labels were popping up to replace the big ones.

Dave Koz's company, Rendezvous Entertainment, was interested in putting out my album, and I began talking logistics with him. I believed my new jazz album could move my career in a positive direction, in terms of both what I wanted to do in the future and how I was perceived by my colleagues in the music industry.

However, sometimes no matter how well you think you've planned the next steps of your career, things can happen to derail you, so you need to always stay flexible. Things didn't go at all as I'd planned.

. . .

In the middle of finishing up my tour with *Joseph and the Amazing Technicolor Dreamcoat*, I had met a young musical entrepreneur, Darius Jordi, who was seeking clients. He had heard through the grapevine that I was now unattached to any record company. Although Darius was involved in several projects based in Los Angeles, he called and left a message for me in Miami, asking if I'd be interested in having him represent me.

I kept putting off returning his call, trying to figure out how to go about organizing and producing my new jazz recording on the heels of completing the lullaby for Dave Koz's project, *Golden Slumbers: A Father's Love*. Finally, I called Darius back and explained my desire to become an independent artist and manage my own career from now on.

"Jon, hear me out," Darius said politely. "I'd like to work with you for a few weeks, no strings attached. Let me outline what I have in mind for you, and we'll see if that might work for you in terms of releasing the record you have now and where to take your career at this point. You're a big name, so you can choose whether you want to sign with a big record company or a boutique label, or stay independent. Will you allow me to work with you for a while?"

I finally agreed. Darius was young, but he was persuasive, and what did I have to lose? I really enjoyed his youth and his entrepreneurial spirit, and he was making it clear that I could explore our relationship without committing to anything. It was that easiness that I appreciated, the lack of pressure, because after ending a relationship with Emilio that had lasted for so many years, I was being careful about what deals I signed on to next.

One of the first things Darius suggested was that he accompany me to the Grammy Awards in Los Angeles, where I was going to be a presenter at the pre-telecast show. "If you don't mind," he said, "maybe we can take some meetings in L.A."

"Okay, that would be fine," I said, and true to his word, we went to the Grammy Awards and mingled. I saw several faces I recognized from SBK/EMI, people who had moved on, including the president of EMI publishing, Martin Bandier, whose job was still going strong. He gave me a warm greeting and I introduced him to Darius.

Martin said, "Jon, so good to see you. Why don't you come to the EMI party after the Grammys? You'll always be part of the family."

It didn't feel that way to me, since I hadn't heard from anyone at his label after SBK closed its doors. I understood why, though. Nobody had intended for things to go this way, but literally, one day their doors were closed, and the relationships among all of us were unique, so special and then so disappointing in how they ended that nobody wanted to be reminded of what had been. Certainly nobody—including me—had wanted to be put in a position where someone asked what was going on in your world, knowing that the world as I knew it had just ended. It was a really, really awkward situation, to say the least. Still, the EMI party was always one of the most lavish, and Darius was eager to attend it, so I agreed. By now, I was ready to let the past be past and keep moving forward.

There are a million people at those parties, so many you can barely navigate the crowd. It's a feast of everything the music business represents, both bad and good. You talk to people left and right—artists, producers, executives—with most people wanting to see and be seen because there are cameras set up outside the party. Everyone wants to know what's going on.

This party was in a Beverly Hills hotel, a classic post-Grammy overload, but for me it was wonderful. At this point in my career, I felt I could relax. I didn't have to prove anything anymore. I was just an independent bystander, a recording artist whom people still recognized, and the party gave me a chance to reconnect with colleagues in the music business, many of whom I hadn't seen in years. Meanwhile, Darius was at my side, working the room.

Every few minutes I'd bump into someone I recognized, or who recognized me, and I'd start a new conversation. One of these people, Jason Pennock, was a songwriter and producer who had worked with someone else at EMI. We began talking shop, and he started telling me about independent labels and how the industry was moving in this direction. "If an independent label is well financed," he said, "if the company has the resources to market and promote products, it's a great option for artists."

Jason went on to tell me about his sister, the great singer Joey Daniels, signing with Big3 Entertainment, a small label in St. Petersburg, Florida. "The label's financed by someone who's very passionate about music," he said, adding that Big3 had just signed Cheap Trick.

After Darius and I left the party that night, I flew back to Miami without giving that conversation a second thought. I was busy working with Rendezvous Entertainment, trying to make the deal happen with my jazz CD, which I wanted to be made up of mostly my original songs, along with a few select covers. For instance, it included a jazz version of "Angel." Overall, I wanted the album to have an integrity of concept, and I patterned it after songs done by Johnny Hartman, a jazz vocalist from the fifties who specialized in ballads.

This album felt markedly different from anything else I'd ever done and was truly a labor of love. I was actually tapping into my jazz education and a part of who I was as an artist and musician in a way I'd never been able to do throughout my career. I was making an album that had nothing to do with pop music, but everything to do with my musical integrity based on my roots.

About three weeks after attending the Grammy Awards, I was still talking to Rendezvous Entertainment about a deal when

Darius called me. "Listen, Jon," he said, "I've been thinking a lot about what kind of an agenda to put together for you, but something jumped out at me back at the EMI party. Remember the conversation we had with that guy about this company in Florida? Well, I researched it, and I made a call. If you want to take a meeting with them, we can."

"Darius, what are you talking about?" I asked, bewildered. I'd forgotten about that conversation completely.

To this day, I respect that young musical entrepreneur for having listened to everyone we met and taking notes. Darius knew exactly what he was talking about, and he gave me great advice. "Yeah, Jon, you remember," he said. "The guy whose sister was signed to that company, Big3 Entertainment? I did a little research and he was right, that would be a good label for you. I called them on your behalf, and told them that you're independent now and trying to figure out how to work your career. The president of the company is very interested in talking with you."

As I listened, I thought about the jazz album and the deal I was about to sign. I was on the brink of shutting Darius down, but then I reminded myself that I'd made a vow never to reject an idea before fully exploring it.

"I'm not sure," I said truthfully.

"Look," Darius said, "the company is located really close to you. I'll fly myself from L.A. We'll meet with this company and hear what they have to say. They're making waves in radio, and the backbone of the company is very well financed."

"Okay," I agreed. "Let's set up a meeting."

So we met with the head of Big3 Entertainment in St. Petersburg, and I was impressed. The financing they offered was structured more like that of the big labels I'd come from, only on a smaller scale. It felt like a grassroots kind of company and I liked that. The company was definitely based on the vision of the CEO,

Bill Edwards. Although he hadn't come from the music industry, Bill was willing to hire the right people to make his record company work the best way it could as an indie label.

It was a short meeting held at Bill's corporate office and attended only by Darius, Bill, myself, and the president of Big3, Maryann Pascal. Bill's own commitment to promote a small group of artists by giving them the attention they needed was what finally drew me into making a commitment to Big3.

At the end of the meeting, I told Bill I'd done a jazz record I wanted to put out.

"That's fantastic, Jon," Bill said, "but you're a pop recording artist, aren't you?"

"Yes," I said. "That's what I've always been."

"Well, that's the kind of artist that I want to help you be at Big3," he said. "I want you to continue having your name out there as a bilingual pop recording artist."

"I appreciate what you're telling me, Bill," I said. "But I just finished producing this jazz record and I really want to release it."

"I'll buy it from you," he said. "I'll pay back whatever you spent to produce it, but I really feel like you shouldn't put this album out right now. You can just give me the rights to release it in five years."

Bill also expressed an interest in serving as my manager. I was a little bit apprehensive about that idea, since I'd come into the meeting with Darius. Not being a man who was short on words, at one point Bill asked me directly about my relationship with Darius.

"We're getting to know each other," I said truthfully. "Up to this point, Darius has just been here to help me facilitate my independent career."

Right at that moment, Darius and I both realized where the conversation was going: Bill was going to present what's called a "360-format deal" in the industry, whereby the interest of the company becomes more than just signing you as a recording artist; it includes managing your appearances and publishing career, too.

To his credit, when we left the meeting, Darius said, "Jon, whether or not you sign on with this company—which is an idea I think you might want to entertain—one thing is certain. I have no role in your career. I came into this wanting to see if I could find a way to work with you, but in all honesty, I should step aside."

I appreciated his honesty, and I'll always respect Darius for that generosity and the way he handled our relationship professionally right from the start. We still occasionally talk today, and later on we did work together on some other things. At that time, though, we parted ways with a handshake.

Somewhere in my career, I knew the time, chemistry, and opportunity would be right for me to produce that jazz album. Right now, though, I appreciated the fact that Bill understood what that album meant to me—so much so that he paid me for the expense of making it and put the album on hold, with the promise of returning the album to me if he didn't end up releasing it. I was also grateful for how highly Bill regarded my career as a pop singer and songwriter. As a result, instead of being an independent artist making my own way completely solo, I found myself now signed on with Big3 Entertainment. It was another new day.

B ill Edwards, the CEO of Big3, is unlike anyone else I've ever met in the music industry. He has always loved entertainment with the same kind of passion I do, but he's a very assertive businessman. He was a Vietnam veteran who had started from nothing and built one of the country's most successful mortgage companies, beginning with his desire to help other Vietnam veterans get loans.

Bill was a direct, no-nonsense kind of professional, someone opposed to the sugar coating I'd been used to hearing in the music business. Whatever he wanted to do, he just straight out told you: "This is what I'm doing, and if it doesn't work, it doesn't work." He was a man of few words, but his basic belief was, "I don't fail. I succeeded in the mortgage industry and I will succeed in the music business."

I loved Bill's straightforward nature. He was prepared to take on my career, and I really appreciated his dedication and drive because it matched my own work ethic. We shared a relentless desire to hustle and succeed. In addition, I knew that my career would be a priority at his small boutique label, and working with them would give me the opportunity to balance my life the way I wanted to as a musician with a family. We immediately started working on our first pop record together, *Same Dream*, and we would go on to do five in all, three in English and two bilingual productions.

Big3 was housed in the same building where Bill had his mortgage company. He had established a full-fledged studio there, one of the best I'd ever seen in my life. I still compare it favorably with any other studio I've ever recorded in, when it comes to quality equipment and production. It mattered a great deal to Bill that his artists had the best possible facility.

For *Same Dream* album, I had to come up with a whole new repertoire. As we worked together I fully realized the beauty and significance of a well-put-together production company. I was able to hire a collection of guys I knew in Miami to help me write and produce the songs, including my old friend Miguel Morejon, who gave me the first single, "Window to My Heart."

It meant the world to me that we could finally use "Window to My Heart." Miguel and I had written it in our usual way, through a series of conversations we'd had while I was floundering through the relationship with Ana and starting to get to know Mari. We'd always liked the song, but it had been sitting on our demo shelves for a while. Imagine our thrill, then, when that song ended up being another Top 5 hit in Adult Contemporary for us! I was ecstatic about that.

Miguel and I never did go out to celebrate that success properly—or any other, come to think of it. We were both too low-key for that. But for my fortieth birthday party, Miguel did something really cool. He brought me a giant gift-wrapped box, and when I tore off the paper, I saw that he'd given me a unique present, so meaningful that I couldn't take my eyes off it: the battered old boom box he had rigged so that we could hear the sequences we were creating for "Just Another Day." The speakers still sounded like crap. And I still have that boom box in my house today.

We produced that first album quickly, and I was able to meet directly with the team Bill had hired to distribute it. He had even crafted a distribution deal with EMI, again showing me how flexible a small outfit could be. I really appreciated having the opportunity to work with a company that was willing to promote my music. Having done this myself for *Amanecer*, I knew what it took for an independent company to make any song a Top 5 hit as they'd done with mine.

Bill also introduced me to a network of new venues for my concerts, like resort casinos. All in all, it was a wonderful time for me, because now I could balance songwriting, producing, and doing shows. It was also a steep learning curve, as I began to fully embrace the idea that artists no longer had to sign with huge record companies in order to create, distribute, or promote songs. It was possible to outsource all of the major elements required to get your music out there.

In creating *Same Dream*, I was able to bring to the project all of my many years of experience. The process was made especially smooth by the fact that I recorded the album at Bill's incredible studio in St. Pete, a laid-back city where I had none of the usual distractions. I was able to take on the role of executive producer and oversee things while Bill's team did the hands-on work, and I came away from the project thinking this was exactly the way I wanted to work from now on, with an enthusiastic team in a state-of-the-art studio completely isolated from the rest of the world.

By spreading my wings to encompass new possibilities in the indie music world, I had entered not just a new day but a new era, one where I could thrive as an artist. I had stopped stressing about album sales and I'd readjusted my expectations. I was making enough money to support my family as a recording artist and songwriter, doing the work that I loved more than any other while at the same time finding time to have fun with my wife and children.

In re-creating my life, I felt the same kind of excitement I'd felt as a new singer in Miami landing my first singing and songwriting gigs. The world was full of infinite possibilities. All I had to do was keep knocking on doors to see what was behind each one.

CHAPTER TWENTY-ONE
You Can Still Be You on Television

The next door to open surprised even me. Behind it was a chance for me to do one of the biggest reality shows on television.

In 2004, Movistar was sponsoring the first season of *Latin American Idol*, an offshoot of the original British show, *Idol*, and its U.S. counterpart, *American Idol*. FremantleMedia, the show's producer, planned four auditions, in México City, Bogotá, Caracas, and Buenos Aires. The show would air via the Sony Entertainment Television in twenty-five different countries.

I had heard about this new venture, since I was a big fan of *American Idol* and the judges on that show—Simon Cowell, Randy Jackson, and Paula Abdul at the time—had advertised the Spanish-language version in a video. But, until Big3 got a call from the show's producer asking about my availability, it never once crossed my mind that my future might lie in reality television.

Although this was the first time FremantleMedia would be

producing an *Idol* show in Spanish, they had the format down. Its success was virtually guaranteed. Still, they wanted me to audition to be a judge, and I had no idea if I had the kind of quick-thinking charisma that would work on live television.

Neither did the producers. My television experience was limited. I had enjoyed performing on big national shows like Letterman and Leno, and in cameos for shows such as *Beverly Hills 90210*. I'd even appeared in Mexican soap operas. But none of that could prepare me for judging a reality TV show.

The producers were bluntly honest when I met with them at the FremantleMedia offices in Miami. "We're very interested in working with you, Jon," they said. "At the same time, we know you've never had any experience being a judge on television, so we need to see how you fare."

In effect, they wanted to test me on camera, to see how I handled myself when listening to singers and stating my opinions. I just said, "Be yourself," and went to the audition, not knowing what the producers were looking for or expected from me.

What you see on TV is what really happens on an *Idol* show. As a judge, I was expected to give my honest reaction to the singers, so being myself was the number one priority for the show's format. I had two significant obstacles to overcome after I was hired. The first was that I had to deliver my opinions in Spanish—and not the sloppy sort of Spanglish we all use around Miami, that wonderfully entertaining hybrid of Spanish and English, but in classic, grammatically pitch-perfect Spanish that the Latin American viewers would understand. I really struggled with that at first, and had to keep reminding myself to think and speak only in Spanish so that I would grow more at ease.

The second and even tougher obstacle for me to overcome was learning how to be really assertive and sound confident. I've always hated hurting people, and my inclination is to err on the side of being too kind. The producers weren't having any of that.

"Jon," they said in frustration after a few shows, "you, probably more than any of the other judges, bring to the table so many different elements of experience and pieces of advice about the music business as an entertainer, artist, and educator. Everything you say has to sound authoritative and direct."

The producers were on me constantly that first year, calling me out if it ever sounded like I had been second-guessing myself while delivering a critique of one of the contestants. So there I was, on the hot seat every show, knowing that I couldn't ramble and I couldn't sugarcoat my opinions. I had to deliver concise, expert decisions in a matter of seconds—and all in perfect Spanish. And no matter how much I might question whether I should let some talented young singer go when the other judges wanted to keep the singer, I had to stand by my opinion without wavering. Talk about a challenge!

Of course, the contestants themselves made the entire ordeal even more emotional for me. I still remember one show in Venezuela where a young boy got very defensive when we turned him down at his audition. He actually approached the judges' table and stood right in front of me, leaning forward and saying, "Why isn't it good enough? Why?" with this very "I want to kick your ass" kind of face, all while the cameras were recording.

I kept my cool and kept talking to him, saying, "Look, I'm sorry, man, but you can't go through to the next round," until the producers figured they'd captured enough tension on camera and a security guard intervened, but inside I was afraid he might really go off on us.

Still, despite how difficult it was for me to get used to the process of judging contestants, from the first audition, I enjoyed translating who I was as an artist, along with my background in education as a teacher, into a format where I could express my thoughts in front of a live audience. We were expected to be truthful from the get-go, and that's what makes the *Idol* format so successful as a reality show.

As always, from the beginning of my experience throughout the four years I was on *Latin American Idol*, I was a sponge. This was all brand new to me, and I learned something new every day. Whenever one of the producers would come around the corner to tell me I'd blundered again, saying, "Hey, Jon, what you just said out there doesn't make sense in Spanish," I listened carefully. I also watched myself in playbacks so that I could see what worked and what didn't. Soon I developed a technique of writing down fragments of what I wanted to say, exactly the way I wanted to say it, as each contestant performed.

For season one, I was the only international artist hired as a judge, along with Venezuelan actress Erika de la Vega, Mexican singer Elizabeth Peña, and musical entrepreneur Gustavo Sánchez. The Mexican singer Mimi Hernandez came in to replace Elizabeth for the next three seasons, and Oscar Mediavilla came in to replace Gustavo for season four, but the rest of us stayed on.

The show's format called for us to audition singers in different countries around Latin America, including Colombia, Mexico, Venezuela, and Argentina. Despite the grueling schedule, I was grateful for the opportunity to travel and be seen on television across Latin America, since doing so led me to reconnect with my fan base there and had a huge impact on my own career as an entertainer.

I enjoyed hearing talented young singers perform during their auditions. Even more, I loved the process of doing what I thought of as vocal seminars, listening to the singers compete throughout the show and coaching them in front of the camera. I tried to make my comments short, in keeping with the show's format, and soon got a reputation for being extremely honest without being as cutting as, say, Simon Cowell.

The producers had a dilemma, initially, about what was going to be our "Hollywood," the place all of the singers would travel to for the show. I loved their choice of Buenos Aires, despite the distance and the fact that producing the show there meant I'd have to live in Argentina for four months at a time. I had known Gustavo before the show, so we rented a house together in Buenos Aires.

Gustavo stayed in Argentina throughout the filming, but I traveled back and forth every week between Buenos Aires and Miami. This was a long and grueling flight, but definitely worth it in terms of staying in touch with my family. Basically the show would end every Thursday at eight p.m., and I'd have my bag ready so that I could go straight from the studio to the airport for an overnight flight to Miami. I'd spend the weekend with my family and return to resume taping the show by Tuesday morning. I definitely earned my share of frequent flier miles!

Until actually becoming a judge on *Latin American Idol*, I'd had no idea how much complexity was involved in producing a show like that. Before we launched, a producer from Fremantle's home base in England flew over to explain the rules of engagement, the format, and the theory behind the show. This consultant spent endless hours coaching the producers of *Latin American Idol*, as well as talking to the judges.

Despite the fact that I didn't get to meet Simon Cowell, by working with this supervisor from FremantleMedia, I began to understand the essence of what has made Simon's TV persona so popular for so many years. Basically, the format of the show allows judges to maximize their personalities, bringing their own career experiences and influence to the camera from the very first audition through the day a winner is announced.

As I do with everything, I took my role as a judge to heart. It really clicked, knowing how important my job was in discovering and supporting new talent. I brought everything to the table: my experience as an entertainer, my background as an educator, and my career in songwriting and producing. I worked hard to never doubt myself, to always sound assertive and authoritative in my own way, so that I could offer constructive, believable opinions on air.

The process of auditioning, critiquing, and choosing a winning singer happens exactly the way it appears on television. We were expected to offer our opinions completely cold when the singers walked in. That's part of what creates that sense of tension on live reality television in this format: the judges have no idea whether someone is going to be a clown, a good singer, a freak, or just mediocre and immediately forgettable.

As time went by, I gradually learned how to make sure that my opinions were as concise and clear as possible. I gave myself a limit, saying anything I had to say within fifteen seconds, and always speaking honestly and from the heart. It took me a while to be able to deliver my comments succinctly and with authority, and I made a lot of mistakes in the beginning. I don't have an arrogant personality, and I'm not the sort of person who puts anybody down. As an educator, I'm the opposite, always trying to encourage people who are trying their best. I vowed to find a way to make positive comments even about singers who were really bad.

However, before long I realized I couldn't always uphold that vow. It continually amazed me that the same singer could sound so completely different to each of the judges; I suppose that's why there are so many different tastes in music. Still, I couldn't let myself be swayed by what any of the other judges thought about a particular contestant. I had to be true to my own opinion, and as honest and clear as possible about what I was thinking about a given singer's particular performance. That meant I would have to hurt people's feelings at times. I eventually earned a reputation for offering a smiling but a very cold, blunt commentary if a singer didn't deliver.

For me, the most difficult part of the process was when the producers actually lined up the contestants with their personal stories before they sang. Sometimes a person sings well, sometimes she doesn't, and you can't be influenced by personal tragedies or triumphs. It has to be about the actual performance at any given moment. I tried to put blinders on while people were performing, so much so that my colleagues told me they often didn't know what to expect until it was time for me to give my comments, because I didn't telegraph my emotional reactions in advance.

I did develop a tic that stayed with me throughout the show, one the producers loved. Often clips of the show would show this particular habit. The very first time it happened to me, I felt really bad because it was actually in response to a very sweet, soft-spoken Venezuelan kid who came in to audition. I asked him what he was going to sing, and my demeanor, as always, was one of being welcoming, and even comforting.

Then this kid opened his mouth and the most horrific voice came screeching out. My instinct was to laugh. And not just laugh, either, but to howl so loudly that I was embarrassing even to myself. I was laughing so hard that I was crying, and I just couldn't help it. My instinct anytime we heard a really bad singer was to laugh uncontrollably, and of course that's the shot the producers always chose to show.

Although my cold delivery on the show was sometimes compared to Simon's, I had a little bit of Randy Jackson's urban flair in addition to my own mannerisms. I also had my own way of saying "dog" the way Randy did, only in Spanish. As a term of endearment, especially when talking to some of the guy singers, I'd use the word "Papa" to start my sentences, as in, "Papa, I'm telling you, man, you really sang your ass off," in Spanish.

One day, a girl on one of the shows really blew me away. I was so overwhelmed by her talent that I wanted to say something honest that would express exactly how I felt, so I just told her, "Bien cantao!" This was in the middle of my second season and became one of my staple phrases for anyone who really was exceptional. On television, you have to be smart as well as expressive, so I'd save those key phrases for moments when it mattered most, often during the elimination process toward the end of the show.

By the show's second season, when *Latin American Idol* really took off in certain countries, I began to realize how important the show was for me personally. At that point, the show caused my record sales to go up and my concerts to be fully booked anywhere I went in Latin America.

Meanwhile, I had a wonderfully collegial group in my fellow judges. We might have had our conflicts on television, but we understood that whatever we said at the moment to express a difference of opinion, the moment would come and go. After all was said and done, the show would be over and we'd go out to dinner.

Once I began working on *Latin American Idol*, I fully realized what a tremendous opportunity a reality show presented to its contestants. I wish that kind of show had existed when I was growing up. They have become a major vehicle in today's process of discovering and developing talent—something that doesn't exist in the big record companies anymore. However long these kids lasted in the show, they were working their minutes of fame on television and gaining the kind of widespread visibility that would have been impossible when I started as a singer and songwriter. (Of course, by becoming a judge, I had the opportunity to increase my own visibility as an artist as well.)

The singers who really stood out for me during *Latin American Idol* either won or were in the top five. Whether they won or not was often a matter of week-to-week differences in their performances. Sometimes, for instance, I would hear a singer who I thought was a tremendous vocalist and think that person would win the show, but there was always the element of surprise. Someone I'd overlooked could seize the competition by connecting better with the audience than the more talented singer. Often, the performers who succeeded were those who could fight nerves and insecurities. They'd win because they weren't afraid to command the spotlight.

In my own workshops and seminars with young singers, I often talk about my personal experiences onstage as well as what I witnessed while judging *Latin American Idol*. After we talk about the technical issues involved in what someone is doing (or not doing) as a singer, and the nuts and bolts of what is needed to work on your craft, I always talk about how, in the end, it's your fighting spirit and your personality that will help you achieve success as an entertainer. Your confidence will help you deliver the performance you need to connect with the audience.

At the end of the day, all of these personality facets are reflected in your instrument—your voice—and the way you use it. This separates the entertainers who make it from those who don't. You might have the work ethic to be a good entertainer, but you also need the performance persona—or what judges in reality competitions call "the wild card factor."

Being a judge transformed me once again as an entertainer. I had to learn to organize my thoughts better and be more assertive about communicating my opinions. In the end, *Latin American Idol* helped grow my audience as I learned how to use the immediate connection of television to build my fan.

In addition to soaking up everything I could about the process of making a hit television show, I was exposed to contemporary Latin American pop artists I might never have discovered on my own, simply because the young singers were performing their songs on the show. I particularly loved three Mexican bands—Camila, Reik, and La Quinta Estación—because they exemplified the sounds I'd come to love most in pop music and production arrangements.

There are many different ways to write a pop song, but to me, a great pop song has a connection between melody and lyrics that comes across as simple and sincere. If the simple sincerity of that song can reach listeners on an emotional level in a way people can remember, that's what pop music is all about. Whenever I listen to my favorite groups—whether they're from five years or even fifty years ago—the songs that transcend time and continue connecting with people are simple, honest melodies with words you don't forget.

People sometimes dismiss pop music, but the truth is that many, many people's lives are touched by commercial songs. As a writer, I've heard from many fans who offered stories and testimonials of the ways in which my songs touched—or even transformed—their lives. They've shared wonderful anecdotes, stopping me on the street or after a show, telling me how certain songs have really helped them or meant something to them at certain times in their lives—times of falling in love, times of hardship or loss, times of joy. I like to feel that same connection to music when I listen to it, so I understand how important it is to write songs that will reach people's hearts as well as their minds. Whenever I write, I always want to create a song with a good hook, a great melody, and unique lyrics, but I also ask myself whether this song would touch my heart.

Hearing new pop music always motivates me to write songs, and this time was no different. Listening to the singers on *Latin American Idol* inspired me to write songs in Spanish for the first time. Previously in my career, I had always written songs in English, then adapted them into Spanish. Although I've always been bilingual and switch easily back and forth between the two languages, that was just how I'd always done it. Now, after spending so much time in Latin America and listening almost exclusively to songs in Spanish, I had started thinking primarily in Spanish, and that was where I wanted to go in my writing: back to my childhood roots.

Being part of *Idol* had taught me a lot about what it takes to build a career in music—and to keep rebuilding it. As I listened to young singers day in and day out, I realized how much entertainers—myself included—have to accomplish under really tough circumstances. It takes a resilient type of energy to make it as any kind of artist. I'd had my own set of challenges in launching my career, and these young performers would have theirs.

As a performer, you have to keep believing in yourself enough to deal with the pressure of disappointment and uncertainty about what will happen to your career tomorrow or next week or in ten years. That's the nature of the business. To survive, you have to be passionate enough about your craft to be willing to fall, to land on your feet, and to get up and try again every day.

CHAPTER TWENTY-TWO
Express Everything in Your Heart

I released "Same Dream" with Big3 in 2005, then started working on my second original project for them. We had decided the album would be my take on some of my favorite old standards and called it *Classics*. I chose songs that were known equally in Spanish and English, giving my Latin take on an album Michael Bublé or Rod Stewart might have done. We recorded all of the songs in both languages and called the Spanish version *Clásicos*.

It's not ultimately necessary to have a lot of life experience to be able to sing classics and standards, but having said that, I should add that the fact that I'd reached my forties and become a husband and father helped me add a lot of depth to those iconic songs, simply because I brought a more profound understanding of the themes and messages they contained. My reflections on my own life experiences were threaded into the singing and gave the album an added emotional impact.

In fact, every artist brings his or her life experience to a song.

Whether that artist is tackling standards or brand-new pop songs, often you can hear the singer's emotional range as well as the musical one. Now, in addition to bringing my relatively new experiences as a husband and father to my music, I was also able to bring the understanding and emotions I'd discovered while serving others. I have always made it my mission to give back to my community through charitable work and donations, and that dedication is reflected in my approach to making music.

As a Hispanic American who immigrated to this country, I wouldn't be where I am today without the education I got in the United States, and so education is one of the causes dearest to my heart. I've supported philanthropic activities aimed at funding education at all levels, especially arts education. It's an uphill battle to keep arts programs in our schools with funding the way it is. The budgets of our public schools don't always correlate with supporting the arts, and that's the saddest thing of all. I know from personal experience that the kind of joy and confidence that comes from being involved in the arts can help boost a struggling student's confidence and keep that student in school.

In addition to serving on the President's Advisory Commission on Educational Excellence for Hispanics I continue teaching seminars and master classes at various institutions, including Miami Dade College, the University of Miami, and Riverside Community College. I also do charity events to help raise money for the arts whenever I can, most recently with the Bill Edwards Foundation for the Arts.

I've also devoted much of my career to fighting the spread of AIDS, beginning early in my career as part of the Lifebeat, an organization spearheaded by SBK executive Daniel Glass, and later on with Broadway Cares.

Children, too, command my philanthropic energy. I've done a lot of work with the Make-A-Wish Foundation through the years, as well as being actively involved with Miami Children's Hospital.

One of the most recent philanthropic efforts that made a lasting impression on me was in 2006, when for the first time since childhood I traveled to my native Cuba. Bill Edwards and Big3 Entertainment had arranged for me to perform for the troops stationed at the U.S. Naval Station on Guantánamo Bay.

Even though the location was on the farthest end of Cuba from where I grew up, as we landed in Bill's private plane I felt my eyes well up. I couldn't believe I was setting foot on Cuban soil again, and it was surprisingly emotional to do so after so many decades away. Touring the base and entertaining the troops was educational and rewarding. Someday, I hope, the political standoff between Cuba and the United States will be resolved, so that I can finally show my children where their family originated.

After the trip to Cuba, I did a record of Christmas standards with Big3. Once again, we recorded the project in both English and Spanish. In English, it was called *A Christmas Fiesta*; in Spanish, *Una Fiesta Navideña*. Still, even as I was working on those projects to fulfill my contract with Big3, deep down inside, I continued wanting to put together an original pop album in Spanish. I had started writing songs in Spanish while finishing up my work as a judge for *Latin American Idol*. I was slowly collecting songs, switching gears between Spanish and English as I worked.

By the end of my fourth year on *Idol*, I was no longer signed with Big3. We had completed our contract. Now I faced another big life decision: was I finally ready to fly completely solo, without even the protective safety net of a boutique label?

The answer was yes. I had a great relationship with Bill and with everyone else at Big3, but the time had come for me to produce my own work as an independent artist.

I had started working with a well-known writer and producer from Colombia, Jose Gaviria, after his stint as a guest judge on *Latin American Idol*. He and I come from similar backgrounds;

Jose had lived in Miami for a while, and continued to commute between Miami and Colombia, where he was a judge on a reality TV show of his own—a Colombian version of *X Factor*. Jose had been doing that show for years, and we happened to meet just as I was contemplating a break from Big3 and writing new songs in Spanish.

By the time I became independent, my work with Big3 had led me to be very aware of the many pieces necessary to put a project together. I'd learned a great deal about organization, financing, and outsourcing. Now I felt ready to use what I'd learned to produce my own album.

I had learned, for instance, that the range of how much a record costs to produce has gone down dramatically through the years. The new technologies available mean that it is no longer necessary to record music in a big studio if you're working with the right people. I knew that I could finance my own project.

Bill had never released my jazz CD, so I acquired the rights to that again. I was excited. This felt like exactly the right time for me to be showcasing another side of myself. I still loved that album for what it represented about my roots as a jazz singer. Now, while I was still writing songs for my next Spanish CD, I decided to go ahead and finally create my own independent production package to release it. My time with Big3 had taught me that it was possible for an artist to produce and promote an album without the backing of a big record company, and that in fact that path might be preferable in this day and age. For the project to be a success I just needed to assemble the right cast of people and be willing to risk financing it myself.

Throughout the process of releasing the jazz album, *Expressions*, I had worked with Frank Fiore, a management consultant I knew here in Miami who is also the musical director for Joel Grey. With his help, I decided the best means of releasing the album would be to go completely digital and release it on the Internet.

I hired Michael Caprio to be my publicist and help me create a promotional campaign. I wanted to do as many interviews as I could in the mainstream media. In essence, I was seeking a crash course in social media. I hired the Phoenix Group on Frank's recommendation to help me put together everything from my Web site to my Facebook page, as well as a YouTube page and Twitter, which turned out to be my most valuable outlet of all. Finally, I found a webmaster, Mark Ansman, who had first created a Web page for me when he became a fan of my music twenty years ago. Through all of these steps, I began harnessing the power of the Internet to connect with fans and get my music out into the world.

I enjoyed the process of putting together the social media campaign and spent nearly eight months promoting *Expressions*. In addition, I decided to design a show that would cater to this new recording. But here I was stymied. What kind of show should it be? Up until now, my performances had been high-energy, pop-oriented shows, and now I had this very delicate, acoustic, organic, sultry jazz record.

Suddenly the idea came to me, thanks in part to my stint as the emcee in the Broadway production of *Cabaret*: I would design a show I could do in cabaret-style rooms! This would allow me to put on more intimate productions and return to my club days, which I'd always enjoyed. I was excited to design a show that would recreate for me the essence of the intimate musical environments I'd first started working in as a club singer in Miami during college and graduate school, a time when all of my performances were with small, organic, acoustic ensembles. Now that I had so much more experience as a producer and a performer, I was sure that I could deliver shows that were even more personal and entertaining for a variety of audiences by working small rooms in a casual, unplugged atmosphere. My lifelong goal has been to connect with listeners. Now it was a refreshing thought, frankly, to realize that I didn't have to do a big pop show with computers; I could just strip down to the barest, most beautiful essentials of a musical performance.

Once I hit upon this idea, Frank did something for me that I will always be grateful for: he connected me directly with Joel Grey, asking Joel to come to one of my rehearsals as I was putting the show together to showcase the jazz CD. Amazingly, Joel agreed to coach me and help me make it the best show possible.

Joel was a master at cabaret shows, so this was a real honor for me. In person, Joel was a sweetheart. He arrived wearing slacks and a sweater, looking just like a regular silver-haired older man, despite the fact that he'd been in countless theatrical productions and was doing a show of his own in New York at the time. He gave me a hug and said, with an air of absolute sincerity, "I'm here to help you, Jon. Let's do this. Let's go to work."

And, boy, did we work! He guided me through the structure of the show and every piece of the material. It was like taking an intensive college course with a master performer. Or, maybe more accurately, I felt like a child in school learning from one of the most incredibly gifted, passionate entertainers in the history of theater. Joel immediately extended to me that certain camaraderie I'd felt from other performers on Broadway that comes from giving so much of yourself to the show and the audience that you surrender who you are as a person to pay homage to the art of entertainment. Joel was completely present, feeling my passion and stopping me at intervals to demonstrate or tell me something, critical at times but in such a nurturing, endearing way that I felt like we were putting together a puzzle as a team.

I've always been the sort of person who likes to break down whatever I'm told and analyze it to make sense of things. Together, Joel and I broke down that show. He was especially instrumental in helping me think about how the environment of playing in smaller, intimate rooms meant I'd have a more transparent connection with people in the audience.

One of the main lessons I learned from Joel that day is this: even if something looks improvised onstage, it shouldn't be. Being a professional entertainer requires you to work everything out ahead of time, designing every word, laugh, and gesture you'll do in front of an audience. There can be no throwaway moments, especially in intimate venues. You must pay attention to details and rehearse those details. To this day, no matter what kind of show I do, I blend a little bit of that kind of cabaret-style intimacy into my performances.

I was nervous, of course, that I wouldn't be able to pull it off. Who was I, without the computers and lights, the big band behind me? I had to struggle the first few times not to let my nerves show. Thanks in part to Joel's coaching, the shows were a success. Meanwhile, I continued working on my next Spanish project while grappling with the reality that my father, who had always been my mentor and was forever ready to support me any way I needed it, had fallen ill. In fact, he had been sick for a long time—longer and more seriously than I had suspected.

By 2009, as I was working on the jazz CD, it was clear that my father didn't have much time left to live. Once again, I was reminded of his message: happiness is never permanent. Just when you think life is smooth sailing, here comes another tsunami.

My parents have always been completely supportive of me and my career. In part, they demonstrated this support by never talking to me about anything regarding their own health, because they didn't want me to have to worry about it. They put my career and life at the forefront of their own priorities.

In my father's case, when he first told me he was suffering from hepatitis C, he downplayed the diagnosis despite the fact that he was rapidly becoming sicker. He hadn't been aware of the existence or the severity of this disease, and therefore he hadn't had it diagnosed or treated until relatively late.

My parents had first told me that my father had hepatitis C around 2004. By then, my father was already in his late seventies and had been living with the disease for some twenty years. Honestly, at that point I had no idea how serious hepatitis C could become and what it could do to you if you lived with it. Unfortunately, this disease is one of the silent killers. Not enough people know how to protect themselves against it or have the awareness to be diagnosed early and treated effectively.

My father's illness progressed rapidly after my parents told me he'd been diagnosed. By the time I was approached by Merck and the American Liver Foundation a few years later to be a spokesman for increasing awareness of hepatitis C, my father was nearly blind from glaucoma and severely ill. Hepatitis C, if untreated for long enough, can cause your liver function to shut down; once my father's liver failed, the rest of his organs were affected and his body began to quit.

The American Liver Foundation wanted me involved in their education campaign—just as they'd involved Gregg Allman and Natalie Cole—to put a Hispanic face on the disease. I don't have hepatitis C myself, but the idea was for me to work with my dad on the campaign. At that point, I was smack in the middle of dealing with my father's illness. He was at the doctor's all the time and going through a really tough time with his condition. In the end, he was too sick to help with the campaign.

While battling the illness, my father stayed very strong and spiritually aware, especially when it came to talking with me about anything and everything, from God to my family and career. I will never forget his last days and what he said to me.

Dementia can be a huge side effect of liver failure at that level, and my father's mind was slipping. Nevertheless, during his moments of acute mental awareness when I was visiting him, he would often make spiritual references. Even during his last days in hospice, he enjoyed talking with me about spirituality. He made it clear that I needed to nourish my spiritual strength more than ever, now that I had responsibilities as a husband and a parent. My father wanted to make sure I was okay, and that I was spiritually strong enough to take over as a family leader who would live according to my principles and values.

Finally, I realized that my father was clinging to life because he wanted so desperately to continue supporting me. "Everything is going to be okay," I told him. "I'm going to be okay. I'm ready to take over. How about you? Are you okay? Are you ready to go?"

And my father's last words to me were, "Yes, I'm ready."

I had given my father permission to let go of life on earth and move on. He died shortly after that, on October 31, 2011.

I came home from the hospital in a shambles, but I didn't tell my children about my father's death right away because it was Halloween, a holiday they loved more than almost any other. I wanted to protect them from the turmoil of my own emotions instead of ruining their special day, just as my parents always tried to do with me. I did the best I could to conceal my feelings from the kids that night. The next day, I told them about their grandfather's death, remaining composed as I did so, rather than breaking down. It was yet another way I could honor the memory of the man who'd sacrificed everything to give me a good life, and whose words of wisdom I carry with me everywhere I go.

More than any other refrain, I like to think of the lyrics I used in "I'm Free," the words I borrowed from my father about "a rainbow shining over us in the middle of a hopeless storm," and how I'm free, because "things are only as important as I want them to be." He was a wise man, my father. I was lucky to be his son, and even now, I feel his love like a rainbow over me.

Sometimes, your performance as an entertainer is elevated during life-changing moments, when you experience a certain synergy between what you're going through personally and what you're doing professionally in front of an audience. The day after we buried my father was one of those times.

I had a performance scheduled here in Miami, at Miami Dade College, arranged long before I'd known my father was going to die. I could have very easily told the directors of the college to call off the show, but I knew my father wouldn't have wanted me to do that. Despite my raw emotional grief, I decided to perform as a way of honoring his life.

I won't ever forget that particular show, because it brought full circle so much of who I am in relation to my spiritual connection with my father. That performance was a reflective one; at first, I thought I would never get through the night, but instead I rose to the occasion, and for that show I brought everything in my history as an entertainer, my balance of character and career.

It was a wonderful performance, but also an emotional one. At one point I got choked up, but everyone in the audience knew what was going on, and I could feel the swell of their support buoying me through the moment. My music, along with the energy of the audience, carried me through that ocean of grief and left me safely on the shore. In my father's memory, I was able to do what I love to do, expressing everything in my heart through song.

CHAPTER TWENTY-THREE
The Joy Is in the Journey

My experience as a judge on *Latin American Idol* led me to appear on other reality shows. Some of those experiences were positive, but others were less so; I learned a great deal from all of them. In fact, I probably learned more from the mistakes I made than from the shows that went well, because it is only in making mistakes—and figuring out how to recover from them— that you can test your flexibility and resilience as an artist and as a person.

One of the shows, *Divas*, was based in Peru. This was a reality singing competition featuring only female performers, and I enjoyed a few months as a guest judge there. I also joined *Yo Soy*, a reality show in Chile. Once again, I loved having the chance to mentor young singers and hear pop songs I hadn't yet had the opportunity to discover in the United States.

A far less enjoyable experience was my stint as a competitor on the first season of *Mira Quién Baila*, the Latin version of *Dancing with the Stars*. I was invited onto the show by Mario Ruiz, a dear friend and, at the time, the artistic director of Univision. He and I go back many years, because he used to be at EMI; I was the first person Mario thought of as they launched the show in September 2010.

Mira Quién Baila started with a huge ratings bang and was an immediate success for Univision. I loved being on the show because I was learning so much. However, I've rarely been as anxious as I was while competing on that show every week. I'm not a dancer by profession, but of course in my perfectionist world, I wanted to do the best I could.

Every week was a challenge, since I had to get into a new mindset and learn a different dance. I wanted to do the dances justice, and my partner, too, because I respect dancers so much. Dance is an art form that requires complete commitment. It's a beautiful artistic expression of emotion that combines music and motion.

I was doing fairly well on the show—I think I was one of four or five remaining contestants—when I had an accident unlike anything that had ever happened on the show before, or since. As I had done a million times in rehearsal prior to showtime, I took my partner and lifted her over my shoulder from the floor. She was supposed to land on top of my thigh at the end of the move.

Unfortunately, my partner landed on my knee instead of my thigh. I took all of her weight on my kneecap and felt it pop. It was excruciatingly painful; I tore my anterior cruciate ligament (ACL) and my medial collateral ligament (MCL), and I dropped my poor partner, who fell on her back and hit her head on the floor.

My instinct, despite the fact that I was splattered all over the floor, was to try to get back up and at least create the fantasy that I was still okay. But I wasn't. My left knee was so badly torn that I had to be taken away from the studio by ambulance and quit the show. My partner underwent tests for head trauma, but to my relief she was fine.

Since the show was so popular, the accident was replayed on television over and over again. I was mortified. However, I got nothing but love and concern from my Hispanic fans. The first thing out of anyone's mouth was, "How is your knee?"

I was very thankful when doctors told me I would heal physically with the right physical therapy, but it was more difficult to heal my bruised ego. Mari was in the TV studio watching the show when I fell, and my daughter had also been watching and cheering me on. I felt terrible and embarrassed for letting them both down.

My next thought, of course, was how I could speed up my recovery. But I sought to get back on my feet as fast as possible, no pun intended. I wanted to put the accident behind me and forge ahead. The secret of success for any entertainer is to take situations that aren't in your control and make the most of them. You have to put your ego aside and capitalize on whatever you have going on in your career. I told myself, "I'm better than this injury," and kept going.

I didn't miss a beat. I made physical therapy part of my everyday workout routine so that I could get back onstage stronger than ever. I had a big show coming up at the Magic City Casino, and I was determined to be ready for it. I performed with a brace on my knee, but I made it. The show must go on, and I made sure it did!

By 2010, I had wrapped things up with Big3, issued my jazz CD, and immersed myself in social media. I'd proven to myself, as well as to others, that I definitely had all of the pieces I needed to put together recording projects independently. I had been collecting songs in Spanish for several years along the way. Now, at long last, I was finally ready to produce my first Spanish album, *Otra Vez*.

I had decided to bring in a production partner to share both the work involved in the project and some of the financing. I could have gone the route of hiring a management company to work on my behalf and sell my product and career to a big label, but when I balanced my ambition against the thing that matters most to me in life—my family—I realized that doing so would tilt that balance in a way where I'd have to make sacrifices in my personal life I simply didn't want to make.

Instead, I resolved to manage my own career. I could stay as busy as I wanted to be, and do things by choice. The important thing would be that I'd hold the reins to my own future from this point forward.

It always pays to stay on good terms with the people you work with in the music business, because things have a way of going full circle. Now I chose to create a partnership with someone I'd met twenty years before, Hans Reinisch. Hans was a former EMI executive, so I thought he'd be the perfect combination of someone who knew my history and the status of the music industry.

Together we organized a strategy for producing and promoting *Otra Vez*. Our partnership lasted a couple of years, for the purposes of that record and some other marketing scenarios we worked on. It was a risky partnership in the sense that I'd never done anything like this before, so it would be a huge learning curve for me, as Hans and I tackled everything from production to marketing and tried to figure out which pieces of the production puzzle I could handle myself and which tasks we really should outsource, even though they might be costly. This was also my first foray into using social media as a marketing tool.

The thing about being an independent artist is that there is a great deal of freedom to think outside the box, and that's great. But you also have to shoulder all of the financial responsibility, which can be anxiety-provoking. You can never risk more than you can afford to lose. I'd seen firsthand how certain albums could plummet without ever getting any traction. That could happen to me again. At the same time, I also knew that I was truly ready to start a new day as an independent artist, and I needed to have faith in my own abilities.

Working with Hans was like a scaled-down version of working with Big3, but our basic strategies were very similar. We put the album out on iTunes using our own distribution label, hired a publicity firm to help with promotions, and used a radio promoter to get my songs on Spanish radio.

To my relief, the project was a fantastic success. *Otra Vez* was distributed here and throughout most of Latin America. I'm still receiving royalties from the different countries where we brokered deals, and I learned that there are immediate rewards if you succeed as an independent artist. While of course the process was easier for me since I was already an established entertainer, I still found it educational and enlightening to see that if you know how to organize a marketing campaign and outsource, you can achieve success with a record album. The songs got enough airplay for me to realize that I wanted to continue working as an independent artist.

My career has now reached a point where everything is intertwined. Producing *Otra Vez* led me to travel and experience a new wave of attention as an entertainer. I also began exploring other entertainment avenues as an independent artist. For instance, I entered into a great partnership with the Magic City Casino here in Miami, where I opened my own lounge. I was flattered by this opportunity because it's a big casino in the middle of Miami; they approached me knowing I was a local kid who had grown up to become a successful entertainer.

Working with the casino has been fantastic. I consult with the management on booking talent for events and concerts, as well as doing my own concerts there. For our opening, I was excited to work with Olivia Newton-John and perform songs from *Grease*, a show with music we had both performed before and still loved. Olivia is a great artist and a star in every sense of the word. I had done a couple of benefit shows with her for her foundation, so she was gracious enough to accept my offer of performing at my new casino bar.

The key to building a lifelong career in the entertainment business remains the same as it ever was: keep your eyes open for new opportunities, nurture your friendships, don't be afraid to take risks, and remember to count your blessings and say thank you at the end of the day.

My development as an entertainer continues to parallel my emotional growth as a man. Like the music industry, marriage and parenthood change day by day, even minute by minute.

After my father died, my mother surprised us all by taking over the hands-on tasks of managing the properties that she had helped him invest in through the years, showing us her vibrant energy and business acumen. She is as strong-willed and opinionated as ever. If Mom doesn't like something I'm doing, she lets me know about it.

Mari, too. As our children become teenagers and we see their personalities developing, we realize they have the same sense of spirit and passion as we do. My son is a combination of Mari's family and my mother, while my daughter is definitely showing personality traits that both Mari and I share, including a love of the arts.

In my family life, as in music, I continue to try to be a better communicator. Just the other day, Mari and I had a disagreement when I came home to find her locked in a raging argument with our daughter about her use of the computer and cell phone. Mari tends to be a strict disciplinarian, and her personality is very confrontational, even somewhat militant, while I still have that same tendency to perhaps be too laid-back, letting things go rather than laying down the law.

In this instance, we got really heated, arguing over what was best when it came down to establishing social media rules for our daughter, who's now in high school. "Listen, can we talk about this separately for a minute?" I asked Mari, because we've tried to establish a habit of arguing somewhere away from the kids—a holdover from my own youth, where I hated seeing my parents fight.

In the bedroom, I started talking calmly, but as things got more heated I rose to a boiling point. Still, if there is one person who can get me there faster than anyone else, it's my wife, until I have to step up to her level and argue just as ferociously as she does. This last time, the conversation escalated to the point where I was screaming at the top of my lungs and so was Mari. When I scream, I start breathing so hard it's like a workout at the gym.

When Mari heard me start screaming, she suddenly just stopped arguing and broke down. She cried like I never saw her cry before.

"Maybe I'm failing at this," she said.

I took her in my arms. "You're not," I said. "You're a tremendous mother. You're okay, and so am I. Our family is a good one."

It hurt her to see me lose my temper, and it hurt me to see Mari like that because she normally has such a strong sense of self.

At the end of the day, though, recovering and rebuilding your relationship after arguments, like re-creating yourself after upheavals in the music industry, makes you stronger, more resilient, and more determined to do better next time. Mari has been a true partner, sharing the passion and challenges of every aspect of my personal and professional life.

The essence of being a successful entertainer is to let your instincts take over and revert to where you came from. In my case, I came from the ground up, and I'm glad I did. My inner core of confidence comes from the same deep-rooted mentality as an immigrant who is open to embracing change and endless opportunities, just like my father, who always looked forward despite having to make painful sacrifices, like being away from his family, so we could have a better life.

People like my parents, Mari, and the Estefans have shown me that there is no time for sulking when things don't go your way. Nurture your relationships, pick yourself up if you fall down, and take joy in the journey. Even if I had to open a coffee shop and make Cuban coffee to pay the bills, at the end of the day I would still be enjoying writing songs and singing them.

EPILOGUE

The music world is small. I've always tried to conduct business in a way that allows me to keep building relationships rather than burning bridges. It's important to me to reach back over the past twenty years to work with people I've known in the past. You never know when it might come in handy to call on an old friend or colleague.

Right now, for instance, I'm back in the studio with my old friend Rudy Perez, working on new songs in both Spanish and English and collaborating on specialty projects. He and I also have conducted workshops for young talent, hoping to inspire and develop young artists.

It has been a breath of fresh air to reconnect with Rudy. I'm always happy to sit down and spin out new ideas and projects, including songs that will become part of my own repertoire. Everything is a work in progress, and one project always leads to another. Meanwhile, I'm still very much in touch with Emilio and Gloria Estefan, and my old high school friend Miguel Morejon recently contacted me to say, "Jon, it's been a while since we actively sat down and worked the way we used to. Want to give it another go?"

I did, and so Miguel and I have joined forces again, writing and producing songs that we can shop around to the many talented young entertainers who reach out to us, looking for new material.

I've also started working on an exciting new stage show with Big3 Entertainment and Bill Edwards. I'm thrilled to be teaming up with Kenny Ortega on this project as well. It'll be a show with an ethnic beat, representing my crossover career as a Hispanic American, performed in both English and Spanish. There will be a story line and great visuals—in other words, everything I've talked about in this book, but in story form.

And what is my story, at the end of the day? It is one of a proud working-class musician from Miami who loves to entertain.

When I look back on my career, I wouldn't change a thing. I love the relationships I've had, and continue to have. Everything I've done—even the mistakes I made along the way, and the changes in the music industry that led to the bottoming out of my career at SBK—led to me to this point in my life, to being blessed and productive, loving and loved. I am as dedicated to making good music as ever, and the music I make is a reflection of who I have become as an artist and, more importantly, as a man. Although I've learned a lot, I keep learning and taking new risks, knowing that's a part of my continued evolution as a person and an artist.

I am passionate about the things that really matter to me, with my family foremost. My father's death brought that to light, along with my new vow to stay spiritually aware and to live life according to the values I hope my own children will carry forth, along with the young artists whose lives I might influence.

Whether I am performing onstage or talking with someone one-on-one, I am determined to be transparent, to be in the present and to be as honest as I can be about who I am as an artist, a father, a husband, and a person. Especially over the last couple of years, the filters have gone away.

I'm completely fine with that. At this point in my career, I thank God and my family and friends for my success, and more than that, for the opportunities I've had to reinvent myself, to recreate my career as an entertainer in many forms, and to continue sharing my love of music with the world. I wake up every morning knowing that it's a brand-new day, one where I'm excited to embrace everything I'm learning to stay passionate and relevant as a performer, while honoring my family and the music I love.

Whoever you are and whatever your passion might be, may you find wisdom, strength, and resilience for each new day.

ACKNOWLEDGMENTS

The final result in all that this book means to me has been an enlightening, educational, and humbling experience. I was blessed with the opportunity to work with a company and a team of professionals that guided me in making my vision come to light.

Thank you, Jennifer Diliz, for your commitment to making this project a reality.

Thank you to my Celebra/Penguin Group family: Ray Garcia—from our very first meeting, you truly shared in my passion and understood what all of us wanted this book to represent. Kim Suarez—the depth of your curiosity was a timely ingredient that made a big difference in pushing the emotional envelope of my story. Thank you both, so much!! Also, many thanks to the managing ed and production teams for their keen attention to detail and for keeping the book's schedule on track.

Thank you, Omar Cruz. It didn't take long for your eye to capture the sentiment of my book in picture. Thank you, Elvis

Sanchez, my longtime friend and hairstylist, and Maria Laura Carrizo, for my makeup.

Mari Secada—over the years, you continue to be an integral part of so many details in the organizational process of every project I take on. Thank you once again, honey.

Holly Robinson—for me, working with you will forever stand out as one of the most rewarding and significant journeys of my career. Your talent, insight, sensitivity, and work ethic are the thread and needle of this book. Thank you, my friend.

And thank you to my fans for continuing to support the career I still enjoy.